Skills Training

Primary years of schooling ages 8–12

Lindy Petersen
with Allyson Adderley

First published 2002
by Australian Council for Educational Research Ltd
19 Prospect Hill Road, Camberwell, Melbourne, Victoria, 3124

10 9 8 7 6 5 4 3 2 1

Copyright © 2002 Lindy Petersen

All rights reserved. Except under the conditions described in the *Copyright Act 1968* of Australia and subsequent amendments, no part of this publication may be produced, stored in a retrieval system or transmitted in any form or by any means, electronic, mechanical, photocopying, recording or otherwise, without the written permission of the publishers.

Edited by Clare Coney
Text design by Jo Waite Design
Printed by Brown Prior Anderson
Artwork by Cecilia Gunnarsson

National Library of Australia Cataloguing-in-Publication data:

Petersen, Lindy.
Stop, think, do: social skills training: primary years of
schooling ages 8-12.

Bibliography.
ISBN 0 86431 544 9.

1. Social skills - Study and teaching (Primary) - Australia.
2. Social skills in children. I. Adderley, Allyson. II.
Title.

372.83043

Visit our website: www.acerpress.com.au

Contents

Welcome to STOP THINK DO in the 21st century   1

Part 1: Why use the program?
Background of STOP THINK DO in schools   3

Why do children need peer friendships?
What is the value of social skills training?
What skills should be trained?
Who should be involved in training?
What are the criteria for effective school-based programs?
How does STOP THINK DO meet these criteria?
What are the aims of STOP THINK DO in schools?
What are the critical skills in STOP THINK DO training?
How is the traffic light symbol used?
What does the research show?

Part 2: How to use the program
The application of STOP THINK DO in schools   15

In the classroom or group
With parental involvement
For behaviour management
For children with special needs
As a whole school
For peer mediation

Part 3: What is the program?
Social skills program for ages 8–10 years 37
Overview of the program
Outline of lesson content
Resources used in the program
Lessons for ages 8–10

Part 4: What is the program?
Social skills program for ages 10–12 years 117
Overview of the program
Outline of lesson content
Resources used in the program
Lessons for ages 10–12

Appendix
Contents of Appendix 199
Information, assessment and training forms
STOP THINK DO resources
References

Welcome to STOP THINK DO in the 21st century

People who work and live with children recognise that peer friendships are very important for children's personal happiness and their adjustment through later life. Social skills training is a way to develop the *social competence* and *emotional intelligence* children need in order to make and keep friends, and thus to relate better with all people in their lives, including their teachers and parents.

STOP THINK DO is an Australian social skills program for use in schools with children who have social–emotional–behavioural difficulties. It is also designed as a classroom curriculum for all children to prevent such difficulties arising. STOP THINK DO has become popular over the past decade since the initial publication of its training manuals, and is now used nationally and internationally.

This latest manual extends and modernises the program, incorporating current research trends, visual resources, a simplified lesson format and practical suggestions for applying the program diversely in school settings. It is suitable for children aged 8–12, in the primary years of school. A similar manual is available for children aged 4–8 years, in the early years of school. A manual teaching the STOP THINK DO concepts – although not in lesson format – is proposed for children aged 12–16 years, in the secondary years of school.

Lindy Petersen, the principal author, is a clinical psychologist with 30 years' experience working with children, adolescents, parents and teachers in clinic and school settings. The co-author, Allyson Adderley, has considerable experience as a classroom teacher of young children through to adolescents, and as an educational consultant involved in the implementation of STOP THINK DO in Australian schools.

The manual is divided into five main sections for easy reference.

- **Part 1: Why use the program?**

Part 1 contains background to the STOP THINK DO social skills training program, its aims, its multi-dimensional and multi-systems approach, and its critical components. This section also covers research into the program and its results: teachers will be reassured that the effort they put into this program serves a very important purpose for their students, themselves and the broader society.

- **Part 2: How to use the program**

Part 2 describes practical strategies for applying STOP THINK DO in schools for various purposes: in regular classrooms, for special needs children, in small withdrawal groups, as a whole school, for student behaviour management, for peer mediation and for parent involvement.

- **Part 3: What is the program?**

Part 3 contains the STOP THINK DO social skills training program for children aged 8-10 years. It includes an overview of lesson format, content, resources and motivational methods, and 20 complete lessons. Each lesson includes aims, materials required and step-by-step instructions. Colourful traffic light posters accompanying the manual support the training program.

- **Part 4: What is the program?**

Part 4 contains the STOP THINK DO social skills training program for children aged 10-12 years. It includes all of the elements described for Part 3.

- **Appendix**

The Appendix contains information, assessment and training forms, a list of all STOP THINK DO resources and comprehensive references.

All that is needed is your motivation!

Part 1 Why use the program?

Part 1 Why use the program?

Background of STOP THINK DO in schools

- Why do children need peer friendships? — 4
- What is the value of social skills training? — 4
- What skills should be trained? — 5
- Who should be involved in training? — 6
- What are the criteria for effective school-based programs? — 8
- How does STOP THINK DO meet these criteria? — 9
- What are the aims of STOP THINK DO in schools? — 9
- What are the critical skills in STOP THINK DO training? — 10
- How is the traffic light symbol used? — 10
- What does the research show? — 12

Why do children need peer friendships?

Research – and experience – indicates that children need friends to ensure their emotional wellbeing and stability in life. Children with friends feel they have self-worth and are more secure and comfortable with the world. Conversely, children with poor peer relationships are vulnerable to psychological, behavioural and social difficulties including delinquency, criminality, drug dependence, dropping out of school, academic and employment difficulties, low self-esteem and motivation, loneliness, depression and psychopathology of various types. These problems may be evident in childhood and last into adolescence and adulthood[1].

And the suffering is not only personal. Society ultimately bears the cost in financial terms since it provides for the medical, legal and welfare needs of people who are damaged by early emotional and social difficulties. There are also costs in cultural terms, as we lose faith in the younger generation and our ability to steer it in positive directions.

Growing up in today's society, children face enormous pressures which can threaten their emotional and social stability … family breakdown, the availability of drugs, rising crime rates, aggressive media, job insecurity, challenges to authority, racial and religious tension and a very fast pace of life. Many children lack the emotional muscle and skills to handle these pressures, or they lack appropriate role models in their lives. They become victims, and themselves create more victims. Consider the tragedies that have occurred throughout the world in recent years where children who are loners with poor social skills, who are ostracised or mistreated by their mainstream peers, form unhealthy alliances and take revenge on their classmates, parents and teachers, with devastating consequences. Good friends can steer children to more positive ways of dealing with life's stresses and support them through difficult times, for the benefit of the child, family, community and broader society.

In view of the potentially traumatic effects of poor peer relationships, it is very worrying to learn from research and clinical experience that around 10 per cent of school-age children have significant problems making friends, and the figure is even higher for children with disabilities. This means that about three children in an average classroom are at risk of serious damage. And the problem is universal!

What is the value of social skills training?

In response to these serious concerns, programs specifically designed to train social skills in children, and thus improve their peer friendships, have proliferated over the past few decades. Fundamentally, the value and aim of social skills training is to develop emotional–social intelligence and skills in children which will improve their relationships with all people in their lives, and enable them to make and keep friends.

Frequently, the premise of these programs is that poor peer relationships are due to deficits in essential social skills and that children can be systematically trained to improve their social competence and, thereby, their peer friendships.[2] A further premise of effective training programs is that children's social competence – and status – is the result of interaction between the children and the social systems around them at home and school, and that training programs need to involve these systems if they are to be helpful to children in real life.[3]

The specific focus of social skills training may be either or both

- *Therapeutic* for children who already have social problems – to provide them with positive skills, attitudes and strategies to replace their negative or ineffective ones, so they too may enjoy the benefits of good peer friendships
- *Educational and preventive* for reasonably functional children or those 'at risk' of difficulties due to their circumstances – to teach them social skills to enhance their friendships and, thereby, armour and protect them from peer rejection and its long-term negative effects.

While schools are able to conduct treatment programs for children with problems by withdrawing them from classrooms for skills training individually or in small groups, it is important to realise that classrooms are particularly suitable locations for prevention programs. STOP THINK DO is *both* a treatment *and* prevention program for use in schools.

What skills should be trained?

Children with friendship problems are not a uniform group; they have different skills deficits, personality styles (for instance, some have an impulsive and aggressive style while others are unassertive and anxious) and problems (some exhibit externalising or acting out behaviour problems, while others internalise their stress). Therefore, effective social skills training programs need to be individualised to meet the specific needs of children, even if training occurs in group settings.[4]

To achieve this end, a program needs to be *multi-dimensional* and include a variety of techniques that will train a variety of interpersonal and friendship-making skills, thus ensuring the program benefits children with a variety of personalities and problems.[5] The most effective programs incorporate cognitive and behavioural training, and take into consideration emotional-affective factors.

Cognitive–behavioural skills

The major elements in social skills training programs are Cognitive Problem Solving and Behavioural approaches, which are based on sound theory, research and practice. In this combined approach, children are taught

- Knowledge of pro-social strategies for friendship making, and how to think about, evaluate and choose strategies for solving social problems, plus
- How to put their solutions into action verbally and non-verbally, with techniques such as coaching, modelling, role-play, shaping and reinforcement built into the program.

Studies over time into the effects of cognitive–behavioural training programs have shown that they work. Not only do they improve children's current social skills and peer acceptance, but they can also have lasting effects later in life in terms of reducing delinquent and anti-social behaviour, drug abuse, school drop-out rates, suicide, anxiety and depression, while increasing self-esteem, academic success, motivation and social status.[6]

Emotional–motivational skills

While complex affective-emotional-motivational factors that drive thoughts and actions are specific to every child and therefore difficult to control, they need to be considered and incorporated in social skills training programs, to ensure the success of the program when used for diverse groups of children.[7]

For example, children differ markedly in their emotional temperaments or dispositions, and in their ability to regulate their emotional reactions and behaviour in social situations[8]. To be socially acceptable, children need to gain emotional control, particularly of angry, aggressive feelings or anxious, worrying feelings, so they can control their reactions and practise more constructive ways of social interaction. Therefore, social skills training programs need to incorporate techniques for training emotional control skills in children, in addition to cognitive and behavioural skills.

Furthermore, in order to sustain the extra effort and energy required to control their old emotional habits and channel their emotional reactions more positively than in the past, children must be well motivated to do so; they must feel it is worthwhile for their lives. To promote the child's emotional commitment – their motivation to be pro-social – training programs need to incorporate motivational techniques such as

- Setting, achieving and reinforcing socially acceptable goals[9]
- Involving children pro-actively to monitor, regulate and evaluate their progress towards goal achievement and further goal setting[10]
- Arranging positive feedback from others (parents, teachers and peers) when children use their social skills and achieve social goals. This further builds their confidence and motivation to keep trying to be pro-social
- Training in peer groups rather than individually, to build a positive peer culture of helping and reinforcing each other. The power of group psychodynamics may then be harnessed to support and reinforce change in individuals.[11]

Who should be involved in training?

Since children's social behaviour and status are reflections of the broader social context in which they live, a trend towards a *multi-systems* approach in social skills training has emerged. This approach incorporates the view that optimum benefits will be obtained and maintained by including parents, teachers and peers as co-trainers, models and reinforcers of change in children.[12]

Parental involvement

Parents represent a constant, relevant, long-term source of reinforcement to children learning any new skill. They can support a social skills training program in many ways, even when their children have significant social-behavioural problems or disabilities.[13] For example, parents can incidentally teach, prompt and reinforce their children's positive social behaviour in natural settings; plan and organise their children's social life especially in non-competitive, small-group, structured peer activities; steer their children towards non-deviant friends who are good models; themselves provide good models of appropriate social behaviour; and coordinate care-givers, to encourage consistency in approach between the main adults in their children's lives. All these factors will ensure longer-term gains.

Depending on how, where and why the program is being run, parental involvement in school-based social skills training programs may take many forms, from minimal to intensive involvement. They may, for instance, be informed by telephone calls and informative notes, and be brought into conferences and discussions. More involvement includes direct coaching of parents in how to reinforce their children's social skills at home, or even intensive, systematic, training for parents themselves, to improve their parenting, management and problem-solving skills.

For children with significant social-behavioural difficulties, it is advisable to include parents in more intensive parent-training programs. However, this is not always possible in school-based social skills programs. Fortunately, there is evidence that the benefits of social skills training programs for children can extend to the home context despite parents having only minimal involvement in the training program.[14]

Teacher involvement

Like parents, teachers are in an ideal position – as a result of their frequent contact with students – to train social learning and friendship-making skills, just as they train academic learning skills. They can also influence children's choice of peers with whom they interact, and can provide consistent and powerful models themselves for appropriate social behaviour.

Moreover, the school system in which teachers operate has many advantages as a training location for social skills. For example

- A social skills program can be included as a curriculum course, with regular lessons and opportunities for practise and reinforcement of new skills in a natural setting. Such a program actually complements and assists the academic curriculum, addressing in the classroom social-behaviour problems that inhibit learning
- The quality of the relationship between teachers and students is enhanced by introducing social skills programs in the classroom, a pleasing outcome in view of the correlation between early child–teacher relationships and children's social competence with their peers, even years later[15]
- Opportunities for formal teacher training in the program can be scheduled into the school calendar, as well as plans for essential ongoing classroom

consultation and support for teachers using the program.[16] Teachers, like students, need to be reminded, reinforced and motivated.

Peer involvement

Research and experience show that a school environment not only provides frequent opportunities for teacher support in social skills programs, but also allows peer involvement, tutoring and mediation. This is true also for children with disabilities or significant social-behavioural problems.[17]

The benefits of peer involvement in social skills programs include
- Modelling of skills, ongoing social support, and regular opportunities for role-play during training and for real-life rehearsal of new skills in a variety of natural settings over an extended period of time
- The formation of a positive group culture, which values the achievement of pro-social goals, and motivates, reinforces and actively helps individual children achieve their goals, including academic progress
- Although the attitudes of peers toward children who have negative reputations are very difficult to change, involving peers in training programs as models, reinforcers and tutors helps shift peer attitudes, even towards those with negative reputations.[18]

What are the criteria for effective school-based programs?

It may be concluded from the above discussion that school-based social skills training programs should incorporate the following components if they are to have optimal results[19]

- A multi-dimensional approach, training a variety of skills using a variety of techniques, to ensure the program is appropriate for students varying in personality, motivation, skills and deficits
- A multi-systems approach, involving teachers, peers and parents, so gains made in the training program last and are relevant in children's real lives
- A systematic, comprehensive social-educational curriculum for the classroom
- An intensive social skills training program for targeted high-risk/rejected students
- Addressing the emotional and motivational factors that cause children's behaviour, as well as training their cognitive and behavioural skills
- Training and ongoing support for teachers/educators running the program
- Strategic or ongoing use of peer mediation and tutoring
- Strategies to improve academic as well as social skills in view of the connection between them
- Continuation of the program over formative years, especially transition periods
- Extension of training across the whole school
- Involving parents as reinforcers and models of good social skills
- A provision for family-focused intervention/parent training.

How does STOP THINK DO meet these criteria?

STOP THINK DO is an Australian social skills training program originally devised three decades ago in the Adelaide Women's and Children's Hospital as a clinical treatment program for children and adolescents referred with social-emotional-behavioural difficulties affecting peer friendships. It has been adapted for use in the school setting and incorporates all the optimum components for school-based intervention listed earlier.

- It is a multi-dimensional program, training cognitive problem solving and behavioural skills, and incorporating affective-motivational factors
- It is a multi-systems approach, involving teachers, peers and parents
- It may be used in schools as a treatment program with individuals or small groups of children who have social difficulties
- It may be taught directly in the classroom as part of a social skills curriculum, with an educational-preventive focus
- The curriculum program extends over the formative years, and may be utilised across the whole school
- It includes a teacher-training program, encouraging teachers to use STOP THINK DO themselves to manage student behavioural problems and model its positive problem-solving method for students
- It creates a positive learning environment in classrooms, to encourage academic progress, and has been further adapted to use with individual students to improve their motivation for learning, including those with special needs
- It includes a peer mediation program for regular, natural training and reinforcement of students' social skills in the classroom and schoolyard
- It incorporates regular parental involvement, with the provision for more intensive parent training if required.

What are the aims of STOP THINK DO in schools?

- To prevent current and long-term adverse consequences resulting from poor social skills and peer friendships, for young people generally
- To improve the social skills and peer friendships of children who already have problems
- To develop cooperative classrooms, and schools, which encourage pro-social motivation and a positive group culture
- To develop children's emotional intelligence and, thereby, their self-esteem and confidence through increased awareness, skills training and goal achievement
- To empower children by teaching them self-control, decision making and positive actions, while also teaching them responsibility, respect and concern for others
- To develop group skills including active participation, co-operation, organisation and leadership

- To improve relationships between teachers and students, parents and children, teachers and parents, through the use of a common language and problem-solving process, shared goals and regular feedback
- To involve parents (and the extended community if possible) in the training program and thus transfer skills into the family and community contexts.

What are the critical skills in STOP THINK DO training?

The critical skills trained in the multi-dimensional, multi-systems STOP THINK DO program are reflected in the principal author's definition of social skills

Social skills refer to the ability in social situations to perceive social cues, control emotional reactions, organise cognitions and produce behaviours with the motivation to achieve socially acceptable outcomes.

The critical skills trained are thus
- **Social perceptual skills**
  To teach children to pick up visual, auditory and spatial cues that will help them clarify problems and feelings
- **Self-control**
  To hold back and control immediate emotions, so feelings can be communicated appropriately
- **Cognitive skills**
  To think about options in social situations and evaluate their possible consequences
- **Behavioural skills**
  To act appropriately, with both verbal and non-verbal behaviours
- **Pro-social motivation**
  To foster attitudes and goals that are pro-social, so children *want* to use their skills
- **Support of significant people**
  To involve teachers, peers and parents in order to extend the children's new skills and attitudes from the classroom to real life.

How is the traffic light symbol used?

The critical skills listed above are taught via the STOP THINK DO problem-solving process using the universal traffic light symbol to cue the steps. People follow these steps when relating with others, especially in problem situations.

This problem-solving process develops
- Perceptual, self-control and communication skills primarily at STOP (the red light)
- Cognitive, consequential thinking skills at THINK (the yellow light)
- Verbal and non-verbal behavioural skills at DO (the green light).

Children are taught this method for relating to others, and particularly for resolving peer conflicts. Adults then continue to remind and guide children through the method in ongoing peer conflicts. Adults also use STOP THINK DO themselves to manage children's behaviour. This combination of direct skills instruction to children *plus* frequent modelling by adults of the same skills is a very powerful teaching and learning technique.

The STOP THINK DO problem-solving process is outlined below. On the left are the steps to be followed by an adult who has a problem with the behaviour of a child (behaviour management use); on the right are the steps followed by an adult guiding children through a peer problem they are having (social skills use).

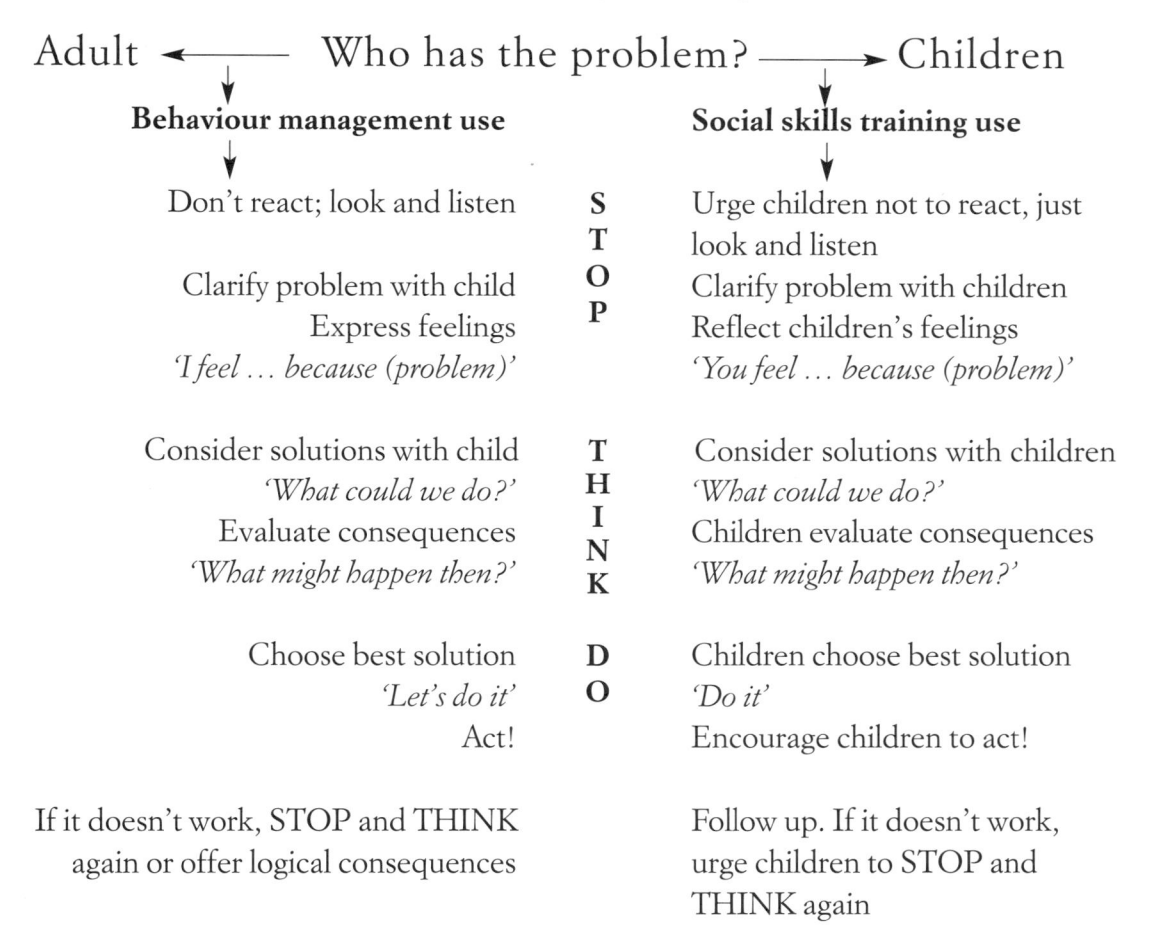

Adult ←——— Who has the problem? ———→ Children

Behaviour management use		Social skills training use
Don't react; look and listen	**S** **T** **O** **P**	Urge children not to react, just look and listen
Clarify problem with child Express feelings *'I feel ... because (problem)'*		Clarify problem with children Reflect children's feelings *'You feel ... because (problem)'*
Consider solutions with child *'What could we do?'* Evaluate consequences *'What might happen then?'*	**T** **H** **I** **N** **K**	Consider solutions with children *'What could we do?'* Children evaluate consequences *'What might happen then?'*
Choose best solution *'Let's do it'* Act!	**D** **O**	Children choose best solution *'Do it'* Encourage children to act!
If it doesn't work, STOP and THINK again or offer logical consequences		Follow up. If it doesn't work, urge children to STOP and THINK again

While the process initially may seem lengthy, it will be shortcut with practice to

'I feel ... because (problem)'	**STOP**	*'You feel ... because (problem)'*
'What could we try?'	**THINK**	*'What could you try?'*
'Let's do it!'	**DO**	*'Do it!'*

For children who have social-emotional-behavioural problems, it is often helpful to consider them as 'stuck' at one of the STOP THINK DO steps. For example

- Dependent, immature children are stuck at STOP; they tend not to think or do much for themselves but generally rely on others and wait for input
- Shy, anxious children are stuck at THINK; they often think too much about what could happen, which prevents them choosing something helpful to do
- Impulsive, aggressive children are stuck at DO; they do and do, and rarely stop and think.

The program aims to 'unstick' children by training them to move comfortably through all STOP THINK DO steps over and over again. In fact, self-discipline, self-control, self-esteem, self-confidence, empowerment, maturity, respect, independence, responsibility – all the ethereal qualities we hope children will develop – are outcomes of using STOP THINK DO whenever and wherever possible.

What does the research show?

The STOP THINK DO social skills program has received support both from formal research studies and considerable anecdotal data over the past two decades.

Educationalists Jan Beck and David Horne (1992) reported on the effectiveness of the program in a special school primarily for secondary schoolchildren with mild to moderate intellectual disability and several with emotional-social problems. The study involved the whole school of 85 students, who were trained in groups of eight, for three sessions per week over a year. Teachers received training in the program prior to and during implementation. Significant gains were reported by teachers, parents and students, particularly in terms of students developing a broader range of social skills, including the ability to verbalise feelings, assertiveness, coping with teasing in non-aggressive ways, keeping friends, thinking before they acted, controlling anger, resolving conflicts with peers and also with siblings at home. Beck and Horne concluded (p. 165) that

> The STOP THINK DO program has grown in popularity as a preventive program in regular schools, as a remedial program in special classes for the emotionally disturbed and as a program for small groups run by specialist teachers ... It has been shown to skill both teachers and students and if parents are involved, to raise their awareness of their child's social strengths and weaknesses, and to assist in improving such skills. On a practical level, it provides useful sequential lesson plans to develop pro-social motivation and behaviour in our students.

An educational psychologist, Joan Nimmo (1993), investigated the effectiveness of the program for enhancing the competence of socially inept primary schoolchildren in Queensland. The study involved three groups of children, aged 7–11 years, who were experiencing social-behavioural problems: a control group receiving no training in the program, a withdrawal treatment group removed from the class for training in small groups by trained teachers and whose parents received a parent training program, and an in-class treatment group whose classroom peers were also trained in the program by classroom teachers but whose parents received no specific training.

The results indicated that the children in both treatment groups made significant gains in key areas of social competence, including making and keeping friends, being accepted by peers, coping with teasing, handling aggression, controlling attention seeking and demanding behaviour, and handling shyness. Sociometric data indicated that class peers rated children in the treatment groups as significantly more acceptable and reported more friendships with them. Moreover, equal benefits were derived for both treatment groups, for children who were withdrawn for small group training with direct parent training and those who were involved in in-class programs with their class peers. The gains showed further significant improvement at three-month review. Evidence for effectiveness across settings was obtained when parents not involved in training reported significant improvements in socially appropriate behaviour at home.

In the United Kingdom, Day, Murphy and Cooke (1999) described a pilot study in a large comprehensive school in Sheffield. Here health and education professionals collaborated to develop an intervention program that would promote the mental health of young people in this region of high unemployment and associated deprivation, and in particular address the high incidence of self-harming behaviours in young adolescents. The specific aim was to teach problem-solving skills to these young people, primarily as a preventive strategy to help them deal better with stress.

Day, Murphy and Cooke worked in partnership with teachers in the school to train students in three Year 8 classes (49 students aged 12–13 years) using the STOP THINK DO problem-solving model. The remaining Year 8 classes formed a control group. The authors concluded that the STOP THINK DO program was beneficial to the participants, resulting in a significant improvement in positive attitudes to problem solving, particularly around problem ownership. Students with emotional and behavioural problems became keen to participate, and listening skills and different viewpoints were encouraged. Particularly successful was the use of a set of traffic lights, manually operated by the students themselves. This was central to the program, helping even those with reading difficulties or from different cultural backgrounds to visualise the problem-solving process. Day, Murphy and Cooke proposed that the problem-solving model should be a framework for health promotion in various areas, including sex education, drug and alcohol use and lifestyle issues that involve making choices. It also represented a workable collaborative venture between health and education personnel to promote the mental health of young people.

A clinical psychologist, Lena Andary (1990), evaluated the STOP THINK DO program in a clinical setting with 25 children aged 7–11 years with identified social difficulties. The results showed a significant reduction in social-behavioural problems as rated by teachers, parents and children themselves at a three-month follow up. Moreover, there was a reduction in clinically significant problems on a standardised behaviour-rating scale. A very high degree of parent and teacher satisfaction with the program was obtained. Andary concluded (p. 24) that STOP THINK DO is a comprehensive package which addresses most of the major issues which the literature reports as being optimal for the acquisition and maintenance of social skills development in children. These factors include a cognitive-behavioural training model with a didactic and experiential approach, a peer group setting and the inclusion of parents and teachers, with … classroom training.

Why? to How?

Having read about the background development, research and aims of STOP THINK DO, we hope teachers and educators will understand *why* the program is useful and feel validated in their choice to use it. The benefits should flow on to their students, school, community and their own lives.

The following section describes *how* the program may be applied in a variety of ways in the school setting, depending on the needs of students, teachers and schools.

Endnotes
1. Hymel et al, 1990; Bullock, 1992; Coie et al, 1995; Ladd et al, 1996; Wentzel & Caldwell, 1997; Pianta, 1997; Asher & Rose, 1997; Bagwell et al, 1998.
2. Coie & Koeppl, 1990; Asher & Rose, 1997; Lawhorn, 1997.
3. La Greca, 1993; Ogilvy, 1994; Spence & Donovan, 1998.
4. Bulkeley & Cramer, 1994; Gibbs et al, 1996; Simpson & Smith Myles, 1998; Matthys et al, 1999.
5. Pepler et al, 1995; Spence & Donovan, 1998; Ladd, 1999.
6. Elias & Weissberg, 1990; Puskar et al, 1997; Frey et al, 2000; Lowry-Webster et al, 2001.
7. Lease, 1995; Cocco, 1995; Thompson et al, 1996.
8. Eisenberg et al, 1997.
9. Parkhurst & Asher, 1985; Asher & Rose, 1997.
10. Kim, 1996.
11. La Greca, 1993; Pepler et al, 1995; Gibbs et al, 1996.
12. Pepler et al, 1995; Harbeitner, 1997; Goleman, 1997.
13. Kazdin et al, 1992; Bullock, 1992; Cousins & Weiss, 1993; Vitaro & Tremblay, 1994; Pepler et al, 1995; Bierman, 1996; Frankel et al, 1997; Lawhorn, 1997; Barrett et al, 2000.
14. Beck & Horne, 1992; Nimmo, 1993; Pfiffner & McBurnett, 1997.
15. Howes, 2000.
16. Farmer-Dougan et al, 1999.
17. Strayhorn et al, 1993; Bulkeley & Cramer, 1994; Pepler et al, 1995; Gibbs et al, 1996; Tankersley et al, 1996; Lowenthal, 1996; Pfiffner & McBurnett, 1997; Spence & Donovan, 1998; Gumpel & Frank, 1999; Kohler & Strain, 1999.
18. Cousins & Weiss, 1993; La Greca, 1993.
19. For example, Strayhorn et al, 1993; Jones et al, 1993; Bierman, 1996; Bierman & Greenberg, 1996; Goleman, 1997; Frey et al, 2000.

Part 2   How to use the program

Part 2 How to use the program

The application of STOP THINK DO in schools

- In the classroom or group   16
- With parental involvement   18
- For behaviour management   20
- For children with special needs   24
- As a whole school   26
- For peer mediation   30

In the classroom or group

In the classroom

Many classroom teachers are interested in improving the way their students relate to each other and also to them. In classrooms where students and teachers relate well, less teacher time is spent on behaviour management and more is available for doing the job for which teachers are trained, that is teaching curriculum. When children are relating well with one other, they will also assist each others' learning; they are less likely to distract others, will notice and reinforce academic progress in their classmates, and will work well in groups. All these create a positive environment, both for learning and for socialising.

The STOP THINK DO program outlined in this manual will achieve these goals for motivated classroom teachers. It offers step-by-step instructions and engaging materials to make the experience a positive one for teachers and students. To implement the program, teachers need the manual, the resources and a plan about when and how long the social skills lessons will run. The program is written in 20 lessons. The course therefore takes a term to complete at two lessons per week. However, the program is entirely flexible in terms of its duration: the number of lessons required, when they are held or how long lessons last is for the teacher to decide, to best meet the needs of the group. For some classes and circumstances, teachers may want to take the program more slowly, by dividing lessons into parts or by extending the whole program over a longer term. For older students or those familiar with STOP THINK DO, progress can be faster through the program.

In addition, classroom teachers are referred to the behaviour management program in this section (pp. 20–23). They consistently need to apply STOP THINK DO themselves when they experience problems with students, thus modelling the process they are teaching the students and so motivate them to use it. Teachers may work through the behaviour management program themselves or, more powerfully, together with other staff.

With individuals or small groups

Teachers or counsellors may feel that some students who have social-behavioural-emotional difficulties need more intensive intervention and training, in addition to, or instead of, the classroom program. The program presented in this manual may still be used with these students, withdrawn individually or in small groups. Such children will have the advantage of more opportunities for individual instruction, skills practice, goal setting and reinforcement compared with a large classroom program.

As in classroom applications, practical issues about lesson times and rate of progress need to be considered by teachers or counsellors withdrawing individual students or small groups from their regular classrooms for training. Again, these decisions are made to suit the particular needs of the students and teachers involved, as long as the program is taught in sequence from beginning to end.

There are also decisions to make regarding the size and composition of the group receiving intensive training.

- With regard to the size of the group, while the social skills program may be adapted for individual training, the effects are not as powerful as training children in pairs or small groups, where there are constant opportunities for peer modelling, shared goal setting and reinforcement, and group motivation.
- Regarding the composition of the groups, it is beneficial to have a natural mixture in terms of gender, personalities and problems, and so mirror the classroom and schoolyard. This provides opportunities for modelling various skills and strategies in the group that will also be valid and workable in the real world.
- In terms of the age range of group members, since the program has a strong cognitive component that correlates with age, the range should be no more than two years. Within this range, students are likely to be able to identify with other group members and develop a group identity that will support change. Implementation of the program is also easier if students move through it at roughly the same rate.
- An alternative application of the program in a group is a cross-age tutoring model. Older students, who are likely to learn the concepts and skills quicker than younger ones, teach and model these skills for the younger group members. Whole classes of various ages may also adopt this cross-age tutoring model by uniting for lesson time.

Teachers and counsellors running a small group or an individual social skills program also need to apply STOP THINK DO themselves when managing student behaviour, and are referred to the behaviour management program in this section (pp. 20–23).

A combined effect

It is important for classroom teachers to be aware of what their students in more intensive, withdrawal classes are learning so that the students' newly acquired skills may be reinforced when they return to the classroom. This means regular feedback between the classroom teacher and the person running the intensive training program. The optimum is when the classroom teacher is also running the program in the classroom. Then the skills of students who are receiving additional training will be positively received back in the classroom. The students will all be talking the same language and reinforcing the 'good bits' in each other. This is particularly valuable for students who already have a negative reputation in the class and school; there is a need for their classmates to change their perceptions of them in a positive direction if the gains made by such students are to last.

The most powerful approach for long-term gain is the application of the program across the whole school, as described later in this section (pp. 26–29). In this situation children with difficulties who are involved in intensive skills training not only receive support for their new skills when they return to their regular classrooms, but also in specialist lessons and the schoolyard, since the entire staff and student body are simultaneously receiving training in the program. The children with difficulties are thus less likely to feel singled out and negative about their training program.

With parental involvement

The degree of parental involvement in school-based social skills programs will vary considerably depending on student age and needs, teacher motivation and support, and parental attitudes and commitment. Essentially, there are three levels of parental involvement.

Level 1: Information feedback and support

For most classroom teachers running the program from this manual, the parents of their students will be involved via an information feedback loop between home and school. This manual provides an initial, introductory letter of contact to be sent to parents (p. 206) and three follow-up letters to keep them informed about their child's progress through the program and how they as parents can assist this progress. Parents also have opportunities formally to examine their child's work through the program, since written and artwork is stored in a tailored Social Skills folder, which gives the program curriculum credibility for parents, students and teachers.

Parents are invited to follow up the information letters they receive with discussions with the teacher. If they require more information on the program or how they may help their child, they may be referred to the STOP THINK DO website at *www.stopthinkdo.com* and *STOP and THINK Parenting* (Petersen, 2002) in the school library.

For more direct support in the classroom program, teachers may actively involve some interested parents. For example

- To assist the teacher in preparing lessons, gathering materials or arranging photocopying if staff are not available for these functions
- To collate pieces of student work during the program for presentation in the school newsletter or the local newspaper
- To discuss the aims and benefits of the program with other parents as members of the parent network; this parental connection may reduce the mystique surrounding programs of this nature for some parents
- To act as co-leaders with teachers during the classroom lessons, particularly when group activities are involved; the suitability of such involvement during lessons depends on the age of the students, and the personality and skills of the parent
- To initiate and maintain contacts in the local community to support the program; motivated parents may
    - approach local business owners regarding displays of STOP THINK DO related student work on their premises
    - write articles for the local paper
    - interest local service clubs like Rotary or local businesses in supporting the program through funding for resources
    - organise fundraisers to help purchase resources and raise the level of awareness in the community of the good work being done at school.

Level 2: Coaching conference

In addition to Level 1 involvement of parents, teachers or counsellors, running classroom or small group programs may involve parents more directly in training and reinforcing their children's new skills. This may be achieved through coaching conferences. An invitation is offered to parents from the class or group to attend a meeting or meetings, to instruct them about the importance of social skills for their child and also things they can do to reinforce the skills being learned at school. These may include

- Strategically using praise for their child's positive efforts, and instituting important consequences when their child does not follow through appropriately
- Providing opportunities for their child to play with other children who are good models of social behaviour and attitudes
- Appreciating the benefits of, and exploring opportunities for, involvement in non-competitive, structured, small group social activities like Scouts, where children can practise their new skills in a supportive, supervised situation
- Explaining to other important care-givers, adults or siblings what the child is learning and how they can extend the benefits of the program by using strategic praise and consequences, and by supporting opportunities for positive social interaction with peers. This develops consistency between care-givers.

Level 3: Parent training program

For parents of children who have more significant social-emotional-behavioural difficulties, involvement in a more intensive parent-training program that runs concurrently with the school program is advised, particularly if the school is putting in effort to organise an additional training program for their children outside the classroom. Since parent–child relationships are often critical in the development and maintenance of more significant disturbance in children, it may be essential for these parents to change aspects of their relationships and management if the child's new skills learned at school are not going to be ignored or, worse, punished at home.

A parenting program includes strategies for improving parents' relationships with their children, and their communication, problem-solving and behaviour-management skills at home. In essence, the parents are involved in a treatment program themselves, where they also receive motivational support from trainers and other group members.

To provide the content for a parenting program, trained teachers/counsellors may work systematically with parents through the *STOP and THINK Parenting* book which contains clear instructions and training exercises. It is economical and supportive to run the parenting program with a small group of parents, meeting on a regular basis through the period when the children's social skills program is running at school. If parents require ongoing or longer-term support, they may be referred to a mental health service or professional in the community.

For behaviour management

To ensure the success of the classroom, small group or individual program, it is vital that the trainers use STOP THINK DO themselves to solve problems they have with students. They need to be models of this effective problem-solving process and of positive self-control, communication, cognitive and behavioural skills if their students are to learn and apply these skills.

To learn STOP THINK DO for managing student behaviour, teachers may use the program outlined below as a self-help tool, or it may be implemented as a formal training program with other staff. For a more thorough explanation, refer to *STOP and THINK Parenting*, which is useful for all adults with children in their care.

The STOP THINK DO behaviour-management steps for adults also follow the traffic light system.

Step 1: STOP, look and listen

Why STOP?

As for children, the hardest step for adults is to STOP their old habits of behaviour management, even if these are not working. Yet there are many reasons adults should STOP first when they are managing children's behaviour; for instance, so they don't

- Buy into too many disputes, or give too much attention to negative behaviour, thus reinforcing it so it is more likely to happen again
- Respond impulsively and emotionally, without thinking, thus providing a poor model of self control to the child
- React to the child personally with put downs and making the child defensive, rather than respond to the behaviour. This is especially true if the child already has a negative reputation
- Talk too much, so that children become too used to the adult's voice and switch it off until the adult raises it loud enough to assault the child's eardrums!
- Make mistakes by assuming they know what happened, or guess on the basis of past experience with the child, rather than find out the facts.

By not STOPPING first when they have a problem with a child, adults often make the situation worse, since the child usually reacts back, using their old habits of defending themselves or getting attention and power. Actually, the problem is not so much the *words* adults say to children but mainly the *tone of voice* they use. Adults generally speak in different tones to different children, depending largely on their own personalities and past experiences with the child; this is why teachers manage some students much better than others!

Of course, teachers cannot be expected to change their personalities or those of their students. Fortunately, by using the STOP THINK DO approach, teachers can avoid reinforcing negative personality traits and bad behavioural habits in their students, since they manage all children in the same way. Individual students are then less likely to take the teacher's response personally or to react defensively, which generally makes the problem worse.

Exercise: *Try the 'Bad habits' exercise in the Appendix (p. 200) to understand what happens when adults don't STOP first when managing children's behaviour.*

How to STOP

The key to the STOP step for teachers is 'Hold back and watch your mouth!' Teachers, however, need to work out their own STOP techniques. These may be

- Step back, sit down, turn away, put their hands behind their back, count to five – whatever it takes to compose themselves
- Look and listen, using their eyes and ears to work out the facts, what is actually happening, including the feelings people have
- Calmly and briefly state the problem and express the feelings appropriately. Use an 'I'-message, such as
  'I am concerned because (the problem)'
  or reflect back the student's feelings, such as
  'You seem annoyed because (the problem)'
- The actual words don't matter as much as the tone of voice; this should stay *low, slow and robotic*, and be the same when addressing all children and all situations. A low and slow voice is calming, and using the same words to all students is not threatening or personal.

Exercise: *Try the 'STOP, look and listen instead' exercise in the Appendix (p. 201). The door is still open for the adult and child to solve these problems.*

Step 2: THINK about options and consequences

If children do not feel that they are being personally attacked for their behaviour, they may adjust this behaviour when it is drawn to their attention in the respectful way described at STOP, without further intervention by the teacher. However, if they don't respond appropriately, move on to THINKING about options for solving the problem with the student or students.

How to THINK

Approach the student or students involved and ask

- How can we solve this problem? What can we try?
- What could happen then? Is that a good idea?

Alternatively, include a larger group or the whole class in the problem-solving process if they are affected. This approach results in less focus on the negative behaviour of particular students, which supports the aims of the social skills program: namely, to identify their 'good bits' and break down negative reputations. For example, if some students leave a mess after an activity, rather than identifying them as 'the problem' and discussing solutions only with them, enlist the class to solve the less personalised problem of *'What shall we do if people leave a mess in our room?'*. The group (including the 'perpetrators') brainstorms options and likely consequences, and then chooses the best option at DO.

The key to the THINK step for teachers is **'Don't be a know-all!'**. Enlist ideas from students, who are learning to use their brains for just this purpose in their lessons. Students will be more committed to, and responsible for, solving problems with teachers if they have an active say in the process. Teachers also need to be open-minded about options, since there is never just one solution, namely theirs! A rule of thumb is to find at least two possible solutions for any problem. The likely consequences will help decide which to choose.

Step 3: Choose the best option to DO

How to DO

The teacher and student or students involved in the process should

- Choose the option that is likely to have the best consequences, either by consensus or a majority vote. If all do not agree, the parties reach a compromise, an option which they agree to try until it is reviewed at a set time
- Work out how to put the plan into action and what needs to be done to make it work.

The key to the DO step for teachers is **'Don't pull the carpet out!'**. Even if teachers are not convinced of the wisdom of the chosen option, if possible allow the plan to be put into action. Students and teachers learn quickly from outcomes. To avoid a sense of failure, however, it is important to set a time for reviewing the outcome.

How to review

At review, reinforce plans that are working well. If a plan is not working well, the people involved go back to STOP and THINK again about what to DO. Alternatively, teachers may cut the process short by offering a choice of implementing the chosen option seriously *or* trying an alternative from the list of options which were first discussed at THINK. For example, if the chosen option for solving the problem of students leaving a mess is not working, the teacher or students may suggest a combination of options: *'Students need to follow the rule agreed on or they will miss out on the next class activity'*, the latter option having been discussed at THINK. It represents a logical consequence of not conforming to the rule. A vote is taken on this option, and a further review time set to check progress.

Exercise: *Try 'Manage the behaviour' exercise in the Appendix (p. 202).*

Benefits of this method

By using STOP THINK DO to manage student behaviour, teachers are essentially 'de-emotionalising' problem behaviour and reframing it as a problem-solving exercise with an individual, group, class or school. Teachers using this method of behaviour management routinely throughout the day reinforce the skills students are learning. The perspective being generated is that teachers and students are on the same team, all listening to each other, all relating in positive and respectful ways, all using skills and a process that works.

Even when students experience consequences of not behaving according to the plan, they are less likely to take it personally, to get upset or angry, and more likely to comply with the consequence because they have been active participants in the decision-making process. They recognise that the same consequences would apply to any student who had behaved in such a way, and they are not being singled out for punishment or blame.

For students who have more difficulty controlling their behaviour and emotions even with the support of the classroom social skills program, teachers may offer additional assistance on an individual needs basis, as described next.

For children with special needs

Individual needs

Children vary greatly in their abilities, their potential to learn new skills and their personalities. While the STOP THINK DO social skills training program is multi-dimensional, incorporating a wide variety of skills and techniques to suit most children, there will be some who need more individual teaching, support and management, to maximise their gains from the program. Some of these students may have identified, diagnosed disorders such as attention deficit/hyperactivity disorder, oppositional defiance disorder, Asperger syndrome or anxiety disorder. Some will be burdened with years of unhappy school experiences. Their expectations of positive change are likely to be low, which naturally affects their responsiveness to social skills training.

Throughout the classroom or group social skills program, all students set social goals and receive positive feedback from teachers and classmates to support their goal achievement. However, children who have significant difficulty controlling their emotions and behaviours often have negative reputations, which make it difficult for other students (and even teachers) to feel comfortable when giving them positive feedback and support. It is very hard to overcome preconceived notions and expectations, and any gains made by these students may largely go unnoticed. While it is the aim of the STOP THINK DO social skills program to change this situation and break the vicious cycle, progress may still be slow and frustrating for these students with extra baggage.

Fortunately, individual attention and input from their teachers may accelerate such students' progress. Utilising a STOP THINK DO framework, teachers work directly with these students to devise and monitor personalised plans for improving their areas of difficulty, either learning or behavioural.

Individual plans

To formulate personalised plans with students, teachers sit down individually with the student and a piece of paper, and follow this procedure

- As in the social skills program, the first step is to identify the child's strengths or 'good bits' (for instance, art, computer or horse riding). This information is gained by observation, discussion with the student, and reports including feedback from classmates in lessons. The teacher draws a line across the page and writes these 'good bits' above the line. Then weaknesses are identified (for instance, listening, maths or controlling anger), again from observations, discussions or reports. The 'weaker bits' are written below the line
- Suggest to the child that he or she has the potential to improve the 'weaker bits' and raise them above the line, to equal the strengths, which are indicators of what the child is capable of achieving. Motivation for change comes from seeing what is possible
- Urge the child to choose one 'weaker bit' that he or she would like to change. It is important to obtain some commitment from the child, even if it is not in the area that the teacher feels is most needed. Students will be more motivated to change if their

choice is listened to, and more interested in pursuing further goals if they first see progress in an area important to them
- The teacher discusses with the student ways to achieve this goal. The actual strategies that might be tried are not as important as enlisting the interest and commitment of the student to engage cooperatively in a plan with teacher support
- A plan is written up using the STOP THINK DO steps, with which the student will be familiar from the classroom lessons. Below is an example of a plan to improve a student's concentration and behavioural control. The student decides which reminders to use to STOP their old negative habits, the actual words they say to themselves at THINK and the specific positive behaviours they will put into action at DO.

A plan for listening and behavioural control

STOP When I see or feel red tape on my pencils (or my friendship band on my wrist or my teacher tapping me on the shoulder), I will STOP and

THINK THINK *'Listen'* or *'Control myself'* or *'What will happen if I do that?'*

Then I will

DO DO the following things
- Stop fiddling, talking, calling out, arguing, fighting
- Listen to or look at my teacher in class to focus
- Go to another place in the yard to keep away from trouble.

Review time: Friday after sport.

- Reminders may be visual (for example, a special sticker on the desk), tactile (a squeeze-ball in the pocket) or auditory (the teacher's voice). When the child sees, touches or hears the cue, he or she is reminded of the plan to improve, and then proceeds to carry it out. Teachers reinforce these efforts. Reminders need to be changed regularly to keep them novel and effective, until the student feels confident in the change themselves.
- A review time is set for teacher and student to meet, to discuss what is working and what needs adjustment. The plan is altered accordingly and a new review time set. Once change has been achieved in one area, another goal may be identified, and a new plan drawn up. Anything is possible when teacher and student work as a team.

Further plans

Examples of individual plans to motivate children to learn and behave well are contained in *STOP and THINK Learning: A teacher's guide for motivating children to learn including those with special needs* (Petersen, 1995). This book describes modified programs for students with special learning needs or disabilities such as dyslexia, Asperger syndrome, attention-deficit/hyperactivity disorder, intellectual delay, or gifted underachievement.

As a whole school

The awareness phase

Identifying the need for – and benefits resulting from – a whole-school implementation of STOP THINK DO is most important if the commitment of staff, parents and students is to be gained. The following strategies may be considered to raise this awareness.

- Utilise surveys and interviews related to the effects of poor social skills on children and the costs to the community, with particular reference to the local area, to make people aware of the need for such a program. The whole school community needs to appreciate these facts and make the decision to support the program
- Consult with the principal and executive-level teachers to discuss the benefits and general aims of the program, together with an example of the STOP THINK DO process
- Present an overview to a whole staff meeting. All staff need to be fully aware of the commitment they are making by taking on the program. Teachers have a heavy workload and already feel burdened by 'add-on' programs. Unfortunately, if this is the perception about STOP THINK DO, it will be soon 'left off'. Teachers need to see the practical benefits for themselves. For example, links may be made with the Personal Development curriculum to identify the areas that STOP THINK DO covers. The program can actually save teachers time and effort in designing lessons for a necessary and, often, mandatory part of a Key Learning Area in the curriculum
- Present an overview to the student welfare team in the school, the parents organisation, the school council and the student representative council. Inform other groups that have a significant input to the school, for instance, the Aboriginal Education Consultative Group
- The student representative council can present the program to the student body via school assemblies, class visits or posters around the school
- Send newsletters and pamphlets home to parents and care-givers outlining the program and its benefits, and enlisting their support. Parents may also be referred to the website *www.stopthinkdo.com*

The planning phase

Once the awareness phase has been completed and there is a high level of commitment across the whole school community, a group may be formed from members inside the school (teachers, students and parents) to drive the STOP THINK DO planning stage, and also to oversee its implementation throughout the school. The particular school dynamic needs to be carefully considered, with sensitivity, open communication and flexibility being shown to suit the needs of the school. The following are considerations when planning the implementation of the program as a whole school.

- Since the program is a school priority, the school management plan needs to allocate the time and resources for implementing the program

- All teaching staff need to participate in STOP THINK DO training and development, including theory and practice sessions. They require training both in the social skills program they will be teaching students and also in using STOP THINK DO themselves as a behaviour-management method throughout the day in the classroom and yard. A day of in-service is required initially, with provision for ongoing support and review sessions for staff as the program is implemented in classrooms across the school. The behaviour-management program in this section of the manual (pp. 20–23) and the teacher-training exercises in the Appendix (pp. 200–203) may be used for staff training, including new staff arriving at the school during the year. Basically, all staff need to be 'speaking the lingo' and 'using the method', to maintain consistency in the whole school management of students
- Time should be allotted for staff to view the program lessons, make adjustments where necessary and identify issues of practical application for their classrooms or group. A realistic timeline for the program needs to be agreed upon by teaching staff
- Nomination of a STOP THINK DO coordinator not only assists with the smooth running of the program but enhances its credibility when coupled with a period allowance. Similarly, a support teacher or teacher's aide assigned to the program can provide practical support with photocopying, and ensure that materials and resources are available for teachers' use
- Maintaining resources in a central location (for instance, in tubs in the school library) is useful for more expensive items like videos that need to be shared between classes
- Pre-assessment of students is advised so that teachers have an understanding of the social strengths and weaknesses of their students, and also a baseline for measuring gains at a post-program assessment. In many cases, changes are subtle and may go unnoticed. It is motivating for teachers to learn that the hard work they are putting in *is* paying off!
- There are advantages in having set times for the lessons running across all classes or, if resources need to be shared, at least scheduled in the same week. For example, this results in
    - students across the school in different grades and classes focusing on the same unit at roughly the same time. Since they 'speak the same language', they can share experiences from their training sessions when they are in the playground
    - staff and students knowing when it is 'STOP THINK DO time' and looking forward to it. This generates informal dialogue
    - training and assistance for casual or relief teachers being easier to arrange, since all classes are running the same lessons at roughly the same time. These teachers can, therefore, deliver the lessons with minimum disruption to students' routines or the whole school program
    - some teachers may need encouragement to deliver parts of the program – the fact that 'everyone is doing it' can provide this encouragement.

The implementation and maintenance phase

While the formal training program is running in the school – and also after its completion – it is vital to maintain the energy, enthusiasm and motivation of staff and students. This needs to be given high priority in the school if gains for students and staff are to be maximised. Some suggestions follow for maintaining motivation during the implementation of the program and the maintenance of gains in the longer term.

- Staff need to receive feedback about the positive results of their efforts. For example, a roster of all teachers may be drawn up and, prior to each weekly staff meeting, the next teacher on the roster will report on a positive change that has occurred at the school since the commencement of the program. This change may be noticed in a classroom, on the sports field, in the yard, on bus duty, on excursions or through parent feedback. The positive change should be noted on the staff display board and discussed at the next staff meeting. It may also be printed in the newsletter for parents, ideally without mentioning specific students
- Weekly assemblies are a good opportunity to share news about the progress of the program. One class presents a brief item each week at assembly, displaying the achievements, activities, role-plays or posters from the classroom program. Parents may be invited
- Student work produced in lessons may be displayed on school noticeboards, and articles and drawings printed in the school newsletter to go home to parents. These may also be sent to the local newspaper to advise the community of the school's commitment
- Parent training may be offered through a behaviour support team, or by a trained teacher or counsellor at the school, for parents of students who have social-behavioural difficulties or are withdrawn from class for intensive training, as discussed earlier in this section. *STOP and THINK Parenting* is a useful resource for this training program, and for the school library as a reference for all parents and teachers
- To organise and implement a peer mediation program in the school, a teacher coordinator needs to be appointed. Set times and resources are allotted for the training and ongoing support of peer mediators, as detailed in the peer mediation program later in this section (pp. 30–36)
- STOP THINK DO's terminology and problem-solving process can be incorporated into other curriculum areas, like health, protective behaviours, society and environment subjects. This further enhances its relevance to students, teachers and parents
- Open days are useful ways of generating enthusiasm for the program, although they need preparation to be successful, for example
    - inviting parents and care-givers way ahead of time … claim that date!
    - inviting the district superintendent or inspector to formally open the day by unveiling a whole-school activity related to the program, such as
        a STOP THINK DO mural
        a STOP THINK DO tapestry or patchwork
        crazy paving, STOP THINK DO style
        paintings of traffic lights strategically placed around the school

- Whole school activities like these can be utilised on an open day or as motivational activities during and after the program. They may be organised by
    - choosing representatives from each class to design a large mural, tapestry, patchwork, paving or painting using the images on the STOP THINK DO posters and other images from classroom lessons
    - requesting volunteers from elective art students at a feeder high school to help supervise and direct the painting/sewing/gluing/paving project. The representatives from each class work with the secondary school 'mentor' on a rotational basis
- To provide feedback to parents as well as maintain parent and student motivation, all classes may demonstrate one aspect of STOP THINK DO according to a timetable made available to parents. The parents can then follow the timetable through the classes and learn about the program
- The school canteen may sell healthy red, yellow/orange and green foods during the running of the program. Some examples are jellies, Smartie biscuits, orange juice, apple juice, tomato, cheese and lettuce sandwiches, spinach pasties with tomato sauce, ice blocks, cheese and capsicum pizzas
- On a particular day, students may be 'out of uniform', wearing red, yellow or green clothing to earn a silver or gold coin donation to a charity selected by the student body
- On a designated Badge Day, the school may hire a badge maker so students can have their prized drawings from lessons made into badges or magnets for the fridge at home
- The STOP THINK DO process should be reflected in the school's student management policy and acknowledged as an integral part of the Personal Development curriculum within the school.

While schools may choose to run the formal STOP THINK DO social skills curriculum in classes for a set period – say, the first term of every year – the skills of the program and the principles of the STOP THINK DO problem-solving process need to be applied at a student, staff and executive level *consistently throughout the year* to maintain the benefits for everyone.

For peer mediation

A peer mediation program in a school involves selected students who have been specially trained, assisting fellow students to resolve social problems in the playground, with teacher supervision. Peer mediators do not judge students or tell them how to solve issues; they listen to them and guide them to cooperative solutions. Because they are peers, they have credibility with students and, because they are well trained, they have skills and motivation to help develop a more positive school culture.

The planning phase

The introduction and implementation of a peer mediation program in a school needs to be well planned. The selection of a teacher coordinator and the students for peer mediation training are important elements of this. The selected students also need to be prepared for their role and the responsibility they are undertaking.

Selection of a teacher coordinator

For the peer mediation program to be successful in a school, there is a need to raise awareness and support for the program, through the school council, parent groups, student body and staff in-service. A teacher nominates for the task of exposing the program to the school community, and also for the role of training, coordinating and supporting the peer mediation program at the school.

A teacher coordinator needs the following

- A belief in the STOP THINK DO program and process
- Knowledge and skills in group dynamics, communication, the mediation and debriefing process, evaluation and feedback to the school community
- Support from the school in terms of time to plan for training sessions, organise resources, conduct the training program and inform the school community.

Selection of peer mediators

A decision is made on the student target group – that is, which students will participate in peer mediation training. Students may be selected by various criteria. For example

- Students in the two senior classes at the school, being nominated by self or teacher
- Students on the student representative council from each class
- A specific number of nominated students from each grade
- Students representing the social, cultural and gender sub-groups of the student body attending the school
- Students who had social difficulties themselves and have some peer credibility – they may also identify more easily with students who are experiencing problems.

Responsibilities of mediators

The teacher co-ordinator has the task of preparing the potential mediators for the responsibility of the role they are about to assume, including being aware that

- Student mediators do not take the place of teachers in the playground and that they will be supervised at all times
- Some disputes are definitely *not* for peer mediation; for example, those involving physical violence, sexual assault or intimidation
- Confidentiality is a serious matter, since some mediation issues may need to be reported to appropriate departments for further investigation
- The coordinator will screen issues before the mediation process begins
- Most mediations will occur during classroom time so that the student mediators' playground activities are separated from their role in disputes. They will not be disadvantaged by losing their lunch and recess time. Disputants are also more willing to participate in mediation to resolve issues if serious (not recreational) time is allocated
- After the initial training program, mediators will organise playground activities for about a term before mediating problems that have arisen in the playground. This establishes their leadership role, gains them respect from fellow students across the school and provides opportunities to refine their communication and mediation skills
- After an official induction before the whole school, where they will be presented with badges and certificates, the students will be identified as STOP THINK DO mediators in the playground – for example, by wearing a distinctive sash or bum-bag
- Following training, mediators will attend regular meetings with the coordinator to identify further training needs, debrief, identify problems and successes, and discuss playground organisation.

The training phase

A STOP THINK DO peer mediator needs to be
- A good team worker
- A good listener, able to identify issues
- A fair person who does not take sides
- A person the coordinator and students can trust
- An approachable person
- Motivated to use the STOP THINK DO problem-solving method
- Flexible, able to deal with a variety of situations
- Able to control personal feelings to remain objective.

Potential mediators need training in social problem solving and mediation skills so that they cope well with the demanding and responsible task ahead. Training may be scheduled over a period of 1–2 days, possibly off site, or over afternoon sessions for a week.

Skills training program for peer mediators

The following table contains the skills required by peer mediators and the activities/exercises that may be used to develop these skills in the training program.

Skills needed	Suggested learning activities to develop these skills
Participate actively in group activities	<ul><li>Co-operative games</li><li>Team-building exercises</li><li>Leadership training</li><li>Assertiveness exercises</li><li>Negotiating a set of rules or a constitution for the peer mediation training</li><li>Practice in introducing partners</li><li>Practice in negotiation of rules during role-plays</li></ul>
Understand the role of mediation in a school context	<ul><li>Define and discuss key features of mediation</li><li>Discuss various types of mediation used in our community to solve problems</li><li>Brainstorm the advantages of having peer mediators in the school</li><li>Discuss examples of conflict in the school that IS and IS NOT appropriate for peer mediation</li><li>Emphasise the need for mediators to be impartial</li><li>Overview the process of mediation and the role the peer mediators will assume</li></ul>
Listen to others, share feelings, ideas and opinions with others, communicate well with peers and teachers	<ul><li>Review main ideas from classroom social skills program where all of these skills are taught</li><li>Discuss mediating role of Bonez in *STOP and THINK Friendship* video and role-play from the script</li><li>Practise identifying and scribing the main issues from group discussions and role-plays</li><li>Practise giving people time to speak and be heard</li></ul>
Apply STOP THINK DO in a range of role-plays	Extensive practice and review of role-plays of conflict situations using the STOP THINK DO mediation checklist in the Appendix (pp 204–5)

STOP step: Listen to both parties Look for body language Control own feelings Identify the problem Identify parties' feelings Summarise main points Be calm, non-judgmental	• Ask both parties to give their version of the problem • Have each party listen to the other without interrupting • Ask both parties how the issue made them feel. Urge them to state 'I felt … because …' • Reflect back the feelings of both parties • Summarise the main points without judgment
THINK step: Elicit options for solving the conflict and likely consequences Accept all suggestions Give accurate feedback	• Ask both parties 'How can you work this problem out?' • Brainstorm possible solutions with the parties • 'What are the possible consequences of each option?' • Clarify these options and consequences for parties without judgement
DO step: Elicit a decision Encourage compromise Reinforce commitment Clarify plan and review process	• Ask parties 'Which option may have the best consequences for both parties?' • Parties choose an option and agree to do it • Mediator suggests 'What ifs' to help parties consider what to do if the plan does not run smoothly • Record the chosen option and have both parties sign the mediation checklist • Negotiate a review date • Thank parties for deciding on mediation

Role-play method

The teacher co-ordinator designs several role-plays to use in the mediator training program which are based on everyday problem issues that can be mediated in the school. Examples may also be taken from the classroom social skills program, the *STOP and THINK Friendship* video (Petersen and LeMessurier, 2000), or the co-ordinator may tape suitable scenarios from television programs. If possible, role-plays are written in the first person to add impact and reality. These situations will then be more meaningful to students practising their mediating skills to resolve the conflict.

During role-plays, student mediators work in pairs for support and reflection; one mediator takes the role of scribe and another leads the disputants through the STOP THINK DO process. It is advisable for mediators to practise the STOP, THINK or DO steps one at a time through the role-play script, and put the process together near the conclusion of the mediation training. The teacher coordinator provides feedback to mediators during role-plays and shapes their style through coaching or modelling.

The maintenance phase

Organising playground activities

Following their training program and induction, peer mediators are involved in preparatory activities around the school before they directly assume the role of mediators in the playground. Over a period of about a term, mediators plan and then implement various activities in the playground. This involvement develops the communication, leadership and problem-solving skills of mediators, and confirms their status as viable mediators to other students.

Suggested activities for mediator planning and involvement include

- Drama activities
- Frisbee-throwing competitions
- Treasure hunt
- Fancy dress
- Balloon games
- Guessing competitions
- Handball, netball, basketball competitions
- Mini fête
- Tug-of-war between classes (including their teachers)
- Birthday announcements
- Karaoke
- Disco
- STOP THINK DO stall.

During these activities, mediators have opportunities to observe and evaluate student interactions in the playground and identify issues that arise for students. With this information gathered over a period of time, mediators can assist teachers in identifying the 'hot spots' and 'hot times' in the playground and suggest how to alleviate stress factors.

This information may be formally recorded, as in the table following.

Our playground today

Date:
Duty area:

Tick the right column for each problem you see and/or a student comes to tell you about.

What problem?	Before school	At recess	During lunch
Pushing, hitting, fighting			
Teasing, name calling, bullying			
Interfering in games			
Swearing			
Out of bounds			
Littering			
Property damage			
Rudeness			
Other (specify)			

This record may also be used as a pre- and post-assessment tool to measure changes in the playground environment following the introduction of peer mediators into the system.

Further information about the organisation and issues of the playground may be gained by mediators presenting surveys to the student body on what students would like to see happen in their playground. These suggestions may be discussed at ongoing mediator meetings, along with considering various ways of implementing such ideas.

The mediation process

When mediators have been involved in playground activities for a while and their status has been identified by other students, they are ready to assume an active mediator role in playground disputes. The student body needs to be advised that disputants may approach a peer mediator or the teacher co-ordinator, to request a mediation and outline the issue to be mediated. This contact could also be made by friends, teachers or counsellors. However, it is crucial for both parties in the dispute to agree to mediation.

A meeting time for all parties during school hours is arranged. The teacher coordinator discusses the issue with the peer mediator before the mediation. At mediation, the parties work with the mediator through the STOP THINK DO checklist in the Appendix (pp. 204–205) to resolve the issue. Disputants may need to be reminded that mediators do not solve problems for students; they assist them through the problem-solving process to reach their own solution.

Debriefing for peer mediators following mediation sessions is essential. Coordinator and mediators discuss issues such as

- How did you feel at the beginning of the mediation?
- How do you feel now?

- Did the parties come to an agreement?
- What part of the process went well?
- What else might have made the process work better?

Ongoing support for mediators

Peer mediators continue to meet with the teacher co-ordinator regularly and often, to maintain their skills and debrief as a team. The following issues need to be resolved to ensure the mediation program runs smoothly in the school and the mediators remain motivated and responsible

- Where will mediators and co-ordinator meet and when?
- How will meetings be conducted?
- What decisions can be made about playground activities from the feedback received from mediator observations and student surveys?
- How will mediators be identified by other students who want to request help?
- How can they maintain their commitment to the program?
- How will they communicate with teachers, parents and fellow students?
- How can they promote the program in the school community?

It is also motivating for peer mediators and teacher co-ordinators to remind themselves that the broader aim of the peer mediation program at the school is to guide students towards a cooperative method for solving issues, and commit them to changing bad habits that have been learned over years in the playground and classroom. A positive whole school culture is being developed and the peer mediation program is an important catalyst.

How? to What?

Having considered *how* to apply STOP THINK DO in various ways in schools, it is time to examine *what* is in the program, the lesson content and methodology.

Part 3   What is the program?

Part 3 What is the program?

Social skills program for ages 8–10 years

- Overview of the program   38
- Outline of lesson content   39
- Resources used in the program   41
- Lessons for ages 8–10   43

Overview of the program

Suitability of students

STOP THINK DO is suitable for children of all ages and all personalities, including shy, anxious, unconfident, unassertive or immature children, and hyperactive, impulsive, aggressive, bossy children, and all those in between. The program presented in this section of the manual is suitable for children in primary school classrooms in Australian terminology, aged 8–10 years.

The program may be implemented flexibly to suit the needs of students and teachers. The length of the program and the rate of progress through it may be varied according to the location and the age, intelligence or special needs of the children involved. For example, younger students, slower learners, those with hearing or language difficulties or autism, or students from different cultural backgrounds, may require more individual attention, repetition, structure or cueing, with the traffic lights and hand signals being adaptable and powerful visual cues. Students with visual difficulties may follow the language cues with tactile representations of the traffic lights and hand signals.

Assessment

Before the commencement of the classroom program, Student and Teacher Pre-Assessment forms in the Appendix (pp. 208–209) may be completed
- To determine the social strengths and weaknesses of the students
- To provide a baseline for measuring progress from the program.

Post-Assessment forms (pp. 210–211) may be administered immediately following the program and/or later for review.

Lesson format

- A requirement for implementing the program in any context is that the sequential order of the lessons be followed through the STOP, THINK and DO steps.
- While the program lists 20 lessons, it is entirely flexible in terms of the number of lessons or duration of lessons. This is decided by teachers to suit their group.
- Each lesson contains
  - the specific aims of the lesson and materials required
  - a brief review of the previous lesson's concepts or skills
  - the structured teaching of a new core concept or skill
  - a related activity, such as a game, role-play, written exercise, discussion or video
  - an alternative activity or exercise for older children in the age block or those already familiar with the core concept or skill.
- Exercises or other work related to social skills lessons are stored in Social Skills folders made up by students before the program starts, to give it curriculum validity.
- At the completion of each of the STOP, THINK and DO sections, an information sheet is provided for parents.

Outline of lesson content

STOP units

Units 1, 2 and 3 focus on STOP, the hardest step of all, signalled by the red light. The main skills taught at STOP are self-control and perceptual skills. Children are taught
- To hold back so they don't react emotionally and use bad habits
- To use their **eyes and ears** to work out the problem and the feelings people have.

These units also contain group-building activities to promote a cohesive, positive group culture which motivates students to learn and use social skills, and particularly to put in the effort to STOP their old habits and control their emotions.

THINK units

Units 4 and 5 focus on THINK, signalled by the yellow light. The main skills taught at THINK are cognitive problem solving and consequential thinking, so students
- Use their **brains** to think about possible options to try with others
- Evaluate possible consequences of these options.

While the emphasis is on teaching children how, not what to think, they learn that some options have better consequences and are worth trying. To identify and describe options quickly, they learn shorthand terms: Cool, Weak, Aggro, Friendly and Cooperative ways.

DO units

Units 6 and 7 focus on DO, signalled by the green light. The main skills at this step are decision/choice-making and behavioural skills. Students learn
- To choose the option with the best consequences
- To act on it, fine-tuning the **body** to send the right signals.

The behavioural techniques used to teach these skills in the lessons include modelling, shaping and role-play.

Techniques for developing pro-social motivation

Techniques for motivating children to learn and then apply the STOP THINK DO skills and problem-solving process are built into the program in various ways.
- Activities and exercises to promote group cohesion, the idea that 'we are all in this together', 'we all want to use our new skills' and 'we help each other'.
- Students identify and set goals for themselves and others, monitor progress towards goal achievement, and reinforce achievement in themselves and others.
- Emphasis is placed on the positive aspects of all people in the class, their **'good bits'**. This often represents a reversal of focus within class groups where 'students with problems' or 'problem students' are well known and often receive negative attention. Students drop this habit as they begin to identify with the pro-social group goals.

- There is formal and regular reinforcement of the 'good bits' of all group members, through activities like posting positive messages to designated classmates (such activities may be incorporated into social skills lessons or used at other times).
- A time is set for daily class meetings, say 15 minutes after the lunch break. Children and teachers sit in a 'social circle', which visibly reinforces the group culture. This is a time for informally acknowledging progress in students, doing a formal 'good bits' activity, planning group projects, or for solving problems that affect the group (such as teasing or bullying) using STOP THINK DO. Even after the completion of the formal training program, the social circle may be continued.
- The fact that teachers use STOP THINK DO to manage problems they experience with students motivates students to have confidence in and use the process.
- Students are encouraged to talk to their parents about what they are learning and parents are encouraged to reinforce these new skills and attitudes in the home. Children are more motivated to learn and apply new skills if they feel that these are valued by their parents. Parents also recognise the validity and credibility of the program through its methodological approach and curriculum style of presentation.

Resources used in the program

Traffic light posters

The three posters accompanying the manual illustrate the STOP THINK DO steps. They are introduced separately as the lessons progress and are designed to be displayed vertically (red light on top, yellow below, green on bottom), reflecting an actual traffic light. Students also make personal traffic light posters which may be used in a variety of ways eg. reduced in size and worn as a badge or carried as a reminder.

Stories/role-plays

Social stories and role-playing are essential ingredients of social skills training programs. In the school setting, they provide a relatively inexpensive yet meaningful resource for training myriad skills in students, such as

- Paying attention and remembering details
- Looking and listening carefully
- Being aware of individual differences in people's attitudes and behavioural styles
- Having self-awareness about how others see them
- Identifying and communicating feelings
- Identifying causes for feelings and, therefore, behaviour
- Perspective taking and empathising with others
- Identifying problems and ways to solve them
- Assuming various roles, including ones they may not take in real life
- Practising and fine-tuning skills
- Providing helpful feedback to others
- Co-operation in groups.

All these skills are fundamental to the STOP THINK DO program. In several lessons, students are presented with descriptions of typical social situations and characters with which children of similar age and circumstance can identify. Additional social problem stories are contained in the Appendix (p. 207) for use in lessons or for spontaneous practice and review of concepts and skills at any time. Students can fill out a storyline by brainstorming ideas and/or writing scripts and dialogue for it.

Teachers are urged to present these stories to students in a convincing manner so they can visualise the situation, clarify the issues involved and identify and empathise with the characters. Following the presentation of the story, teachers engage students in structured discussions. Role-plays are devised by teacher and students to provide more impact and also opportunities for skills practice and feedback in a safe environment.

Some students may initially be reluctant to participate in role-plays. However, because the teacher is also utilising motivational techniques throughout the training program to develop a positive group culture, they will soon realise that it is safe and, indeed, rewarding for them to be an active participant in role-playing. Some students may only volunteer for particular roles with which they can identify. However, here is an ideal opportunity for teachers to assign students roles that they are unlikely to assume in real life, ensuring more varied practice and modelling opportunities, which will broaden their skills base.

An alternative option to storytelling that utilises the visual medium for impact is for teachers to tape suitable social scenarios from television programs popular with their students, and present these, following them up with student discussion and role-play, again pursuing the structure recommended in the program.

STOP and THINK Friendship video package

The *STOP and THINK Friendship* video package is an *optional* resource, which does not accompany this manual and is not essential to the programs in this manual. In several lessons, teachers have the option of using storytelling or a relevant clip from the *Friendship* video for discussion and role-play. However, while it is not essential, the program is greatly enhanced by the *Friendship* video, which was developed specifically to use an appealing visual medium to demonstrate the STOP THINK DO steps to children in a powerful way.

The video package contains

- Real-life scenarios of social problem situations with which children of primary-school age can identify immediately
- A humorous set, the Friendship Neighbourhood, where resides Bonez, a young adolescent who guides the characters in the video (and the viewers) through the STOP THINK DO steps for making and keeping friends. Bonez has credibility as a mentor and mediator since he once had problems but was helped by STOP THINK DO
- A demonstration of techniques to use *and* those to avoid when relating with peers
- A combination of powerful teaching techniques; direct instruction by Bonez in the STOP THINK DO steps *plus* modelling of skills by the children in the video clips
- Exercises on a CD-ROM and a workbook for photocopying included in the video package, which can extend those provided in this training manual
- The full video script in the workbook where teachers can identify the exact clips for lessons as cited in this manual, and also as cues for role-playing exercises.

Other STOP THINK DO resources

In the Appendix is a list of all STOP THINK DO resources (p. 213) that complement the programs in this manual. Some have been mentioned earlier in this book.

Lessons for ages 8-10

STOP

Unit 1:	**Getting to know people**	**45**
	Lesson 1: Getting to know you and me	46
	Lesson 2: Similarities and differences	49
	Lesson 3: Detective eyes and ears	51
Unit 2:	**Look and listen for feelings**	**53**
	Lesson 4: Liking me, liking you	54
	Lesson 5: Identifying feelings	57
	Lesson 6: Reasons for feelings	61
Unit 3:	**Communicating feelings**	**65**
	Lesson 7: Being positive	66
	Lesson 8: Stop the bad habits	68
	Lesson 9: Reminders to STOP	71
	Parent information 1	74

THINK

Unit 4:	**Solving social problems**	**75**
	Lesson 10: Use your brain	76
	Lesson 11: Cool, Weak, Aggro	80
	Lesson 12: THINK about consequences	84
Unit 5:	**The cool and friendly way**	**87**
	Lesson 13: Thumbs up for Cool and Friendly	88
	Lesson 14: Very tricky moral problems	91
	Lesson 15: Cooperative = Cool + Friendly	94
	Parent information 2	96

DO

Unit 6:	**Doing it!**	**97**
	Lesson 16: Fine-tune your body	98
	Lesson 17: What friends DO	102
Unit 7:	**Dealing with unfriendly behaviour**	**107**
	Lesson 18: Saying 'No'	108
	Lesson 19: Teasing and bullying	111
	Lesson 20: We can STOP THINK DO! Yahoo!	113
	Parent information 3	116

Unit 1: Getting to know people

Aims

- To learn skills for meeting and talking to people
- To introduce and reinforce rules for behaviour in lessons
- To learn more about each other, the similarities and differences
- To increase children's awareness of themselves and how they appear to others
- To encourage positive communication and interaction between students and develop a supportive group environment/culture in the classroom.

Lesson 1: Getting to know you and me

Outcomes
Students learn to:
- negotiate rules and consequences for behaviour
- understand more about themselves and others
- use listening, observing and questioning skills

Resources
Poster for rules
Worksheet 1

Step 1

Social circle

a. Sit with students in a circle and explain:
   We are going to spend some time this term getting to know ourselves and each other better. We will learn how to get on better with each other and make our classroom and our playground an even happier place to learn and play. We will have lessons called STOP THINK DO and they will usually begin with a social circle like this.

b. Introduce rules for social skills lessons. Discuss why we need rules in any group – so everyone has a fair go and a chance to learn and participate. Invite suggestions for rules for our circle, and about what will happen when we keep and break the rules. Encourage all students to contribute ideas for suitable management strategies and to take responsibility for reminding others about the rules and consequences. Encouragement and rewards can be given to those who follow the rules throughout the lessons. If we stick to the rules, we will all enjoy the lessons.

c. Encourage the class to decide on some rules and record them on a poster to remain displayed for all lessons. Rules may include

   - We listen to each other
   - Everyone has a turn to speak
   - Everyone can join in
   - We do not put others down.

Step 2

Activity: Getting to know you

a. Divide the class into groups of three. In each group, student 1 is the interviewer who can also participate in the discussion. Student 2 is being interviewed. Student 3 plays the role of an observer. Hand Worksheet 1 to the observers in each small group.

b. Student 1 asks student 2 an open-ended question, for example
   - What is the funniest thing that has happened to you?
   - What is the scariest thing that has ever happened to you?
   - What is your favourite sport and why do you like it?
   - Do you have a pet and why do you like it?
c. Students 1 and 2 discuss the topic for about 3 minutes while the observers check 'yes' or 'no' to the statements on their Worksheet checklist.
d. The activity may be repeated with students changing roles.

Step 3

Discussion: What did you learn?

a. Students go over the Worksheet checklists. How well did they go as interviewers and people being interviewed? Were they paying attention, listening and responding appropriately?
b. What things did they learn about each other that they didn't know before? Ask students to recall information gained about each other from their interviews. Reinforce them for listening carefully, paying attention and remembering details.
c. Discuss broader implications of this activity in terms of rules for meeting and getting to know people generally. These include
   - Approach them directly
   - Smile and say 'Hello'
   - Say your name and ask them theirs if you don't know
   - Ask questions about them
   - Listen carefully to their answers.

These are rules we can apply when we meet people for the first time or talk to people we know a little ... so that we get to know them more.

Teacher preparation: *Collect magazines and newspapers for next lesson.*

Worksheet 1: Observer checklist

Name of student 1   ....

Name of student 2   ....

Name of observer   ....

The observer pays close attention to the conversation between student 1 (the interviewer) and student 2 (the person being interviewed). The observer circles the correct answer.

At the beginning of the interview

Did 1 and 2 greet each other nicely?	Yes/No
Is 1 looking at 2 when they ask the first question?	Yes/No
Is 2 listening to 1 when this question is being asked?	Yes/No

During the interview

Are 1 and 2 looking at each other?	Yes/No
Are 1 and 2 listening to each other?	Yes/No
Are they smiling and looking interested?	Yes/No
Are they sitting still?	Yes/No
Are they asking questions to show they are interested?	Yes/No

At the end of the interview

Did 1 and 2 finish the conversation nicely?	Yes/No

Lesson 2: Similarities and differences

Outcomes
Students learn to:
> be more aware of how others see them
> appreciate people's similarities and differences

Resources
Butcher's paper, glue
Magazines, newspapers
Textas, pencils

Step 1

Social circle

a. Recap rules for social skills lessons and reinforce those who are following them. How can we help those who are having difficulty?
b. Review rules for meeting and getting to know people from last lesson. Emphasise how much we learned about each other, just by asking questions, listening and paying attention. We also learned about things we have in common and things we have different, for example, our pets, what we find funny or scary, and the sports we like.
c. What are other ways people are different? Include race, language and abilities in discussion to suit the age of the group. These differences make us special individuals and make our lives interesting.
d. This lesson focuses on more similarities and differences between us. We will also learn more about how other people see us.

Step 2

Activity: Similarities and differences

a. Students in pairs lie down on large sheets of butcher's paper and each traces the body shape of his or her partner on the paper. Students write their name on the sheet where their own body outline is drawn.
b. Students cut out pictures from newspapers and magazines to identify particular characteristics about themselves; for example, their favourite sports team, food, colours, clothing, cars, animals, television characters. They also ask their partner questions about his or her likes, and help each other find suitable pictures. They work together to paste these pictures on the appropriate body outline. They draw their partner's face on their partner's body outline.
c. These body images may be displayed around the room as a collage entitled 'The class of 200_?'. This is a group building activity.

d. Return to the social circle and discuss the contrasts and likenesses between individuals in as many aspects as possible.

Step 3

Game: Same ... different

a. Students stand behind their chairs. Teacher calls out a specific characteristic and the children who identify with this characteristic sit down. Statements might include 'you are left handed', 'you had toast for breakfast', 'you like rainy days', 'you have a pet bird', 'you love writing', 'you hate computers', 'you are wearing the school colours', 'you think it is okay that we are different'.
b. Discuss how life could be quite boring if we were all the same.

Alternative game: Same ... different

a. A student stands in the middle of a circle of students seated on chairs. He or she identifies something they have in common with one or more students in the circle by observing them closely or looking at their collages. For example, eye colour, shirt, pop group, pet, love of lasagne, favourite car.
b. Those students with that characteristic have to leave their seat and quickly find another seat in the circle, including the student in the centre. The student left without a seat takes the centre position and identifies a further characteristic in common with others. And so the game continues.
c. Discuss how exciting it is that we have differences as well as similarities, because our classroom and our lives could be quite boring otherwise!

Teacher preparation: *Keep some magazines for next lesson.*

Lesson 3: Detective eyes and ears

> **Outcomes**
> Students learn to:
> - listen, look, remember and learn about others
> - appreciate how mistakes are made by not listening
>
> **Resources**
> Detective hat, coat, badge
> Item to be 'stolen'
> Magazine pictures or student drawings
> Paper, pencils

Step 1

Social circle

a. We have learned a great deal about each other in the last two lessons. In fact, we have been good detectives finding out information about each other, getting to know our similarities and differences.

b. This lesson, we will be learning how to use our eyes and ears like good detectives to pay attention to what is happening around us so we don't make mistakes.

Step 2

Game: Being a good detective

a. One student is chosen to be a detective and puts on a hat, coat or badge, and leaves the room. Another student is chosen to be the 'robber' and is given the 'stolen' item to hide. The other students are instructed to look carefully at the robber and describe him or her in detail, so later they will be able to answer the detective's questions without looking at the robber; this would give the game away.

b. The detective re-enters the room and asks a question of each student until the robber is identified. The questions must be able to be answered by 'yes' or 'no', for example
   - Is the robber a boy?
   - Has the robber dark hair?
   - Is the robber wearing joggers?
   - Does the robber have a uniform on?
   - Did the robber hide the item in their pocket?
   - Does the robber sit in the front row of our class?

c. Encourage the detective to listen carefully to the clues and to look carefully at all students, to match the clues to the robber. When they feel they know who the robber is by a process of elimination, they guess. If wrong, they continue to question students until the robber is identified. Repeat the activity with other detectives and robbers.

d. Emphasise how we can easily make mistakes unless we pay attention to what is happening around us, and the cues from other people. We need to look and listen carefully like detectives do.

Alternative game: All eyes and ears!

a. Students form pairs. Student 1 chooses a picture from a magazine or their own drawings without student 2 seeing it. They sit down back to back. Student 1 describes the picture to student 2, who then draws the picture, listening carefully to the clues from student 1. Allow about 5 minutes for the description and the drawing. Students swap roles.

b. Both students show their drawings to each other and compare the drawings to the original pictures described. As a group, discuss whether students made mistakes by not listening carefully to the description of the picture, or by not looking carefully enough at the picture in the first place.

c. Discuss with students. Has this ever happened to you?
- Something you said was misheard by others and they got it wrong
- Other people say that *you* don't listen and you get it wrong
- You are talking about something you saw to someone who saw it too, but they describe it quite differently.

Step 3

Discussion: How can you tell?

a. How can you tell if people are really listening to you?
- Where are they looking? Is there eye contact?
- What is their body doing? Are they facing you, sitting still?
- What are they saying? Are they going 'mm' or 'yes' as you talk?

b. How can you get their attention?
- Start the conversation with a greeting and saying their name
- If they seem to get distracted, ask them if they are listening
- Ask them a question rather than doing all the talking yourself
- Finish the conversation nicely.

Unit 2: Look and listen for feelings

Aims

- To learn to use eyes and ears to find out about people's feelings
- To be aware of facial expression, voice tone and body gesture as cues to people's feelings
- To understand reasons for feelings and, therefore, behaviour
- To further develop a positive classroom culture which motivates children to learn pro-social skills and practise them in real life.

Lesson 4: Liking me, liking you

Outcomes
Students learn to:
- identify positive things about each other
- receive compliments
- set goals to improve social skills

Resources
Coloured paper
Scissors, pencils
Display area (board/paper)
Worksheet 2
Photo of each child on card or 4 tissue boxes, notepaper

Step 1

Social circle

a. Discuss the concept of being a detective, using our eyes and ears to find out what is happening around us and also information about other people. This lesson focuses on telling each other about the positive things we have learned about them.
b. Discuss compliments or positive comments. Request some examples of compliments students have been given by others or have given to others.

Step 2

Activity: Identifying 'good bits'

a. Suggest that everyone has something special about them, some 'good bits', something we could compliment them on. Sometimes we neglect to tell others the things we like about them. Often we just say the things we DON'T like about them. Let's find some 'good bits' about each other.
b. Students trace both of their hands on sheets of coloured paper with their name on. They then move about the room writing a positive comment about other students in a thumb or finger shape of the other students' hands. Teacher may give suggestions initially like 'you're good at art', 'you help me with maths', 'you say "Hello" nicely', 'you're a good class monitor', 'you play with me', 'I like your haircut'. Ensure all ten digits are filled on all hands before stopping the activity. Students cut out their hands and attach them to a large display area to remind everyone of their 'good bits'.
c. Discuss
   - What was it like to give positive comments to each other?
   - How do we give compliments to others?
   Smile, look at the person and speak sincerely.

- What do you say when someone gives you a compliment?
  Smile, look at the person and say 'Thank you'.

Step 3

Exercise: What can I improve?

Students form groups of three to identify something that each person would like to improve. Examples might include 'keep out of trouble', be better at maths', 'control my temper', 'make more friends', 'concentrate better', 'get on with my teacher'. Students also help each other with ideas for goals. They record their personal goals on Worksheet 2, to be reviewed in later lessons.

Step 4

Continuing activity: Reinforcing 'good bits' and improvements

a. Encourage students to look for and comment on improvements they notice other students make. These comments may be formally recorded. For example, a photo of each student may be placed on a piece of cardboard where positive comments may be written. Each week, say, three such photocards are placed on the display board for students (and teacher) to record 'good bits' about that student, or things that have improved, until all students have received positive feedback which may be shown to parents.
b. Alternatively, students post positive messages to each other. Four tissue boxes are fixed on the wall and a name placed on each box. Children and teacher record and post messages to these classmates about positive things they have noticed. The names are rotated through the roll, including the teacher's name, so each person receives positive messages regularly. Teachers should read all messages first, throwing negative ones in the bin with no comment. Children usually drop the habit of being negative as they adopt more positive group goals. Written messages may be saved to build a symbol of the new positive group culture, for example as bricks in a wall, leaves on a tree or links in a chain displayed in the room.
c. Teachers can engineer helpful things for less popular children to do (such as carrying some books to the table, helping another child with maths), and then comment on it to the class and to the child through the post or on their photocard. These motivating exercises may be incorporated into formal social skills lessons or conducted at other times during the day, for example, in class meetings 15 minutes after lunch each day.

Worksheet 2: My goals

Setting my goals: Date ....

What would I like to improve in my behaviour, my work or my friends?

1. ....

2. ....

First review time: Date ....

How am I going with my goals?
Have I or anyone else noticed any improvements?

1. ....

2. ....

Second review time: Date ....

How am I going with my goals?
Have I or anyone else noticed any improvements?

1. ....

2. ....

More goals:

What else would I like to improve now?

1. ....

2. ....

I know I can improve anything if I work at it!

Lesson 5: Identifying feelings

Outcomes
Students learn to:
>   develop skills of looking and listening for feelings
>   identify face, body and voice cues for feelings
>   identify a broad range of feelings

Resources
Worksheets 3 and 4
Cardboard, pivot pins
Textas, pencils

Step 1

Social circle

a. Review the previous lesson about compliments and setting goals to improve. Comment on positive things you have noticed some children doing or saying already. Ask 'How does it feel to hear nice things said about you? Do you feel proud, liked, part of the group, comfortable, happy, safe or, maybe, embarrassed?'
b. This lesson we will be detectives on the trail of lots of feelings, using our eyes and ears to identify them. Distribute Worksheet 3 to students. They guess and discuss the feelings portrayed on the sheet of faces. On the board, brainstorm more feelings we can experience, for example, scared, happy, sad, frustrated, bored, sleepy, angry, surprised.

Step 2

Activity: How can you tell?

a. Students form pairs to examine Worksheet 3 and identify the cues that tell us how each face is feeling. These cues will involve
   - eyes
   - mouth
   - eyebrows
   - brow.

   Students demonstrate the face that goes with each feeling on the sheet.
b. To identify feelings, we also look at the bodily gestures including
   - posture
   - proximity to others
   - hand gestures.

   In pairs, students adopt the body position and posture which they think matches each feeling face on the worksheet.

c. We can also identify feelings by listening to people's tone of voice and words. For instance, if they speak louder and in a heavy voice they sound as if they are feeling angry, or if they speak faster and in a high voice they are possibly excited, or if they speak slowly and in a low tone they could sound sad. Demonstrate these examples in terms of pitch and volume of speech to convey different feelings.

d. Ask students to identify how you are feeling when you make the following statements using different tones of voice, pitch and volume.

'Sorry'
    a. Sympathetic tone   b. Sarcastic tone

'At last we won at football'
    a. Excited tone   b. Exasperated tone

'No one cares about me'
    a. Sad tone   b. Angry tone

'What shall I do now?'
    a. Worried tone   b. Offering to help tone

Step 3

Activity: Feeling wheel

a. Each student cuts a 20-cm diameter circle and a pointer from cardboard, which is fixed with a pivot pin in the centre of the circle. The wheel is divided into eight segments and students write a different feeling word in each segment, for example, *sad, happy, embarrassed, scared, disappointed, angry, surprised, worried.*
b. Students form small groups. They spin their wheels and identify a feeling. In turn, they demonstrate to the group the facial expression, body posture and tone of voice or words that match the feeling they spun.
c. Students also recall situations when they felt the feeling they spun.

Step 4

Exercise: Look and listen for feelings

Students complete Worksheet 4.

Teacher preparation: *Collect magazines and newspapers for next lesson.*

Worksheet 3: Feeling faces

Worksheet 4: Look and listen for feelings

The problem You didn't get what you wanted for your birthday.

How are you feeling? ....

Draw your face

How would you sound? ....

The problem A bully says he is going to 'punch your lights out'.

How are you feeling? ....

Draw your face

How would you sound? ....

The problem You forgot your lines in the school play.

How are you feeling? ....

Draw your face

How would you sound? ....

The problem You passed a test you thought you would fail.

How are you feeling? ....

Draw your face

How would you sound? ....

Lesson 6: Reasons for feelings

Outcomes
Students learn to:
  understand the reasons for feelings
  appreciate that feelings vary between and within people

Resources
Large sheet of paper
Newspapers, magazines
Scissors, glue
Box, stories on slips of paper
Worksheet 5

Step 1

Social circle

a. As a group, repeat the Feeling wheel activity (p. 58) with students spinning a feeling and demonstrating how they would look and sound. Or, as a class, review students' responses on Worksheet 4. Check whether students are being good feelings detectives who use their eyes and ears to identify feelings when looking at face and body, listening to voice and words.

b. This lesson deals with reasons for people's feelings (Why they feel like that), how feelings vary from person to person even in the same situations and how one person can have a mixture of feelings at the same time.

Step 2

Activity: Feelings collage

a. In groups, students find and cut out pictures from magazines showing people with various feelings in various situations. They paste them on a large sheet of paper.

b. Discuss how the people are feeling, and what they might be saying or doing. Students then guess what might have happened to make them feel that way, that is, the reasons for their feelings.

c. Although we can't tell from pictures, people can have a mixture of feelings at one time. Ask students to think of situations when they have felt both
   • Sad and angry
   When you missed out on a treat, but your brother got one.
   • Excited and scared
   You are on a fast ride at the fair.
   • Proud and embarrassed
   You are accepting an award in front of the school.

- Pleased and worried
You passed your music exam but think your friend may not.

d. In addition, different people in the same picture or situation can have quite different feelings. For example, one person may be angry and the person next to him may be laughing. Students find examples of people showing different feelings in the same picture on the feelings collage.

Step 3

Exercise: Different people, different feelings
Students complete Worksheet 5.

Alternative activity: Reasons for feelings charades

a. Teacher photocopies the list below and cuts it up into separate one-line stories (or writes stories on cards) and places them in a box. For example
- You are drawing and your neighbour accidentally bumps you
- You are washing dishes and drop mother's best bowl
- You are in school assembly and you burp loudly
- You just got your spelling test back and you got a very low mark
- Your friends ignore you when you ask if you can play with them
- You open a present and find a $20 note from grandpa
- You turn over a rock at the park and see a lizard
- You walk around the house complaining that there is nothing to do
- You kicked the winning goal at soccer
- Your pet dog is lost and you are looking everywhere for it.

b. Students in small groups pick a piece of paper from the box and devise a play around the storyline, out of sight of the class. They then act out the play to the class in mime, without any speech. Their classmates watch carefully and guess what is happening, how the students who are acting are feeling and why they might feel that way.

Worksheet 5: Different people, different feelings

The problem   **You refuse to eat the dinner mother cooked.**

How are you feeling?   ....
How would your mother feel?   ....

The problem   **You're having fun and are very late home.**

How are you feeling?   ....
How would your father feel?   ....

The problem   **You beat your best friend in a test.**

How are you feeling?   ....
How would your friend feel?   ....

The problem   **Your cousin falls in the pool; she can't swim.**

How are you feeling?   ....
How would your cousin feel?   ....

The problem   **Your brother falls over; a boy laughs at him.**

How are you feeling?   ....
How would your brother feel?   ....

The problem   **Your teacher asks you to finish your story writing before you have play time.**

How are you feeling?   ....
How would your teacher feel?   ....

The problem   **Your best friend won't play with you today.**
How are you feeling?   ....
How might your friend feel?   ....

Unit 3: Communicating Feelings

Aims

- To explore ways of being positive and making people feel better
- To understand the causal connection between feelings and behaviour
- To understand the bad habits people use to express their negative feelings to others
- To learn how to STOP the bad habits, control negative feelings and communicate positively
- To use the red traffic light cue and other reminders to STOP.

Lesson 7: Being positive

Outcomes
Students learn to:
- do and say positive things to others
- help others feel better

Resources
Feelings collage (from previous lesson)
Cardboard, Textas, pencils
Messages on cards
Scissors, ruler, dice

Step 1

Social circle

a. Review the skills required to be a good feelings detective.
  - Understand that different people have different feelings ... and that's okay.
  - Understand your own feelings and the reasons you feel that way.
  - Keep your eyes and ears open to pick up feeling cues from others.
  - If you're not sure, don't guess; ask them more questions to get it right.

b. In this lesson we learn more about making other people feel better by doing and saying positive things.

Step 2

Discussion: Making people feel better

a. Using the feelings collage from the previous lesson, students brainstorm ways they could help the people in the pictures to feel better, for example
  - Listen to them
  - Acknowledge their feelings (*'Yeah, I wouldn't like that either'*)
  - Do or say something positive
  - Offer to help if they can.

  Even if we cannot solve problems for other people, especially if it doesn't really involve us, we can help them feel better by using these techniques.

b. We can also make others feel better by responding positively to their requests if they are reasonable. For example, adults – parents and teachers – often ask children to follow instructions or do jobs. You can respond positively by
  - Saying 'Yes, okay'
  - If you're not sure what is being requested of you, ask them to please explain

- Do it quickly and properly so you don't have to do it again
- If you have a good reason for not doing it, discuss it with them.

Step 3

Game: Being positive wins

a. Students in small groups design a board game with the theme of 'Being positive wins'. Each group cuts a square from cardboard and rules it into a 6 x 6 square matrix. About 12 of the squares are randomly selected and coloured.

b. In turn, students throw the dice and move ahead the number of squares indicated. When they land on coloured squares, they take a card from a pile of special messages and follow the instructions which may include
   - You invited the new student from your class to play at your house on Sunday. That's a fantastic start! Move ahead three squares.
   - You and your friend have much in common. Great stuff! Move ahead two squares.
   - You supported your neighbour when he was upset. You were very kind! Move ahead four squares.
   - You told someone in your class that she was good at drawing. Sweet! Move ahead two squares.
   - You helped your younger brother find his lunch box. Move ahead two squares.
   - You stood up for a boy who was being picked on unfairly. Bravo! Move ahead four squares.
   - You ignored your friend today. That hurts. Go back three squares.
   - You pushed in front of a younger student at the canteen and upset her. That wasn't nice. Go back four squares.
   - You laughed when your sister was told off and it was your fault. Nasty! Go back three squares.
   - You argued with your mother about doing the dishes although you had promised her you would do them. Go back one square.
   - You got mad at your teacher when she was trying to explain your homework to you. Go back two squares.

c. Discuss with students how they felt when they received positive messages compared with negative ones, and that it works the same way in real life!

Lesson 8: Stop the bad habits

Outcomes
Students learn to:
- understand feelings as the cause of behaviour
- identify negative feelings in problem situations
- identify bad habits they use with others
- understand the STOP steps

Resources
STOP traffic light poster
Mastercopy 1, pencils, Textas
STOP and *THINK Friendship* video/workbook (optional)

Step 1

Social circle

Last lesson focused on being positive. This lesson focuses on the way we show our negative feelings to others. When we are upset or angry, these negative feelings cause us to behave in negative ways or 'bad habits'.

Step 2

Story/role-play: Bad habits

a. Instruct students to close their eyes and imagine the following story. For more impact, students role-play the story convincingly.

Sam liked to play handball but his friend was away from school and he didn't have a partner. He wanted to join a game with some other children. Sam approached the group to ask if he could play but they just ignored him. He yelled at them and tried to snatch the ball away.

b. Discuss
- How was Sam feeling? Why was he feeling like that? How could you tell?
- How were the other children feeling? Why? How could you tell?
- How did Sam show his feelings? What bad habits did he use?
- Did it make the problem better or worse?
- Do you use bad habits like Sam when children don't let you play?

Alternative resource: Friendship video: Bad habits

Teacher instructions: *Scenes in the video are identified by a number and a page in the 'Shooting Script' of the workbook accompanying the video.*

a. Show students Scene 1 from the video, p. 39 in the script, where Brent is ignored when he asks to play basketball. Stop tape at the end of Scene 1.
b. Discuss this scene
   - How was Brent feeling? Why was he feeling like that? How could you tell?
   - How were the other children feeling? Why? How could you tell?
   - How did he show his feelings? What bad habits did he use?
   - Did it make the problem better or worse?
   - Do you use bad habits like Brent when children don't let you play?

Step 3

Discussion: The STOP steps

a. Fortunately, everyone can change bad habits. They just have to STOP first when they are upset or angry, like cars stop at the red traffic light to avoid accidents. Discuss traffic lights on the roads.
   - Why do we have them?
   - What do the different colours mean?
   - Why don't cars just keep on going when the light shines red?

b. You can apply the same rules to problems you have with other people. Point to the STOP poster. The red light reminds you of the first step to take when you have a problem with someone

   - STOP the bad habits. Don't let your feelings take over. Wait.
   - Look and listen instead. Use your eyes and ears to work out
     What is the problem... What is actually happening?
     What are the feelings... How are all the people involved feeling?
     These are the questions you ask yourself at the STOP step.

c. If the *Friendship* video is available, play the video from Scene 2, p.40, to the end of Scene 4, p.46, where Brent is about to join in the game without using bad habits this time. Point to the STOP poster. Discuss the STOP step Bonez taught Brent using the words in point b. above.

d. Previous social skills lessons have taught us how to look and listen to find out information. Now we can use these skills to solve problems with other people.

Step 4

Activity: Personal traffic light poster: STOP

Hand out copies of Mastercopy 1. Students design their own STOP poster (or generate one on the computer) to store in their folder or reduce in size to make a badge or card which may be laminated and worn/carried as a reminder to STOP.

Mastercopy 1: STOP poster

Lesson 9: Reminders to STOP

Outcomes
Students learn to:
- recognise their bad habits
- practise the STOP steps
- understand and use reminders

Resources
STOP poster
Scissors, pencils, Textas
Paper, cardboard, red paint
Worksheet 6
Worksheet 2 (first review)
Parent Information 1
STOP and THINK Friendship video (optional)

Step 1

Exercise: My bad habits

Remind students how Sam or Brent in the last lesson did not solve their problem by using bad habits like yelling and snatching. We all use bad habits at times. Hand out Worksheet 6 for students to complete.

Step 2

Story/role-play: STOP first

a. In the social circle, ask for volunteers to discuss bad habits they use when they are feeling angry or upset.

b. Fortunately, we can change our bad habits by following the STOP steps. Remind students of Sam's story last lesson. Introduce this element

   Just before Sam asked to play, Sally twisted her ankle. The others were calling to her to see if she was okay. They weren't really ignoring Sam at all.

c. Students form small groups and design role-plays where Sam doesn't use bad habits. He stops first, controls his feelings, looks and listens to find out what is *really* happening and how people are feeling like we learnt to do.

d. In the circle, discuss
   - Did STOPPING first work better for Sam?
   - Do you think it is strong or weak for Sam to control his feelings?
   - How likely is he to forget next time he is upset or angry?
   - He needs much practice at STOPPING so it becomes a *good* habit.

Alternative resource: Friendship video: STOP first

a. Show the video from Scene 5, p. 47, where Brent tries again to join in. Stop the tape at the end of Scene 8, p. 48, after Bonez discusses reminders.
b. Students may role-play this scene to practise the STOP steps. Discuss
- What worked for Brent? (Controlling his feelings, looking and listening to find out what was happening and about other people's feelings – like we learnt to do)
- Do you think it is strong or weak for Brent to control his feelings?
- How likely is he to forget next time he is upset or angry?
- He needs much practice at STOPPING so it becomes a *good* habit.

Step 3

Activity: Reminders to STOP

a. Reminders help us remember things. The red light is a reminder to STOP, control our feelings, look and listen to work out what is happening, just like the red light reminds drivers. Students have their own personal STOP poster from last lesson to stick on their desk or reduce to wear or carry.
b. There are many other reminders they can use, things that attract their attention so they notice it. Students brainstorm ideas for reminders, such as wearing a friendship band or different coloured socks, carrying a special key-ring or toy in your pocket, putting coloured tape on pencils, sticking Velcro on the brim of your hat or displaying the STOP symbol around the play area. Teachers can also be 'reminders' to students by quietly saying something like 'Remember the red light' if children are using bad habits.
c. Students choose a reminder to try for themselves. When the novelty (and hence, its effectiveness) wears off, they choose another reminder until they feel in control of their feelings and behaviour.
d. In small groups, students design and paint small red traffic lights for the yard. They walk around the school to decide where they would benefit from reminders being placed, for instance, on walls, fences, windows.

Step 4

Exercise: Am I improving?

Students refer back to Worksheet 2 for a formal review of their progress towards achieving their goals, as identified in Lesson 4. Students will have received feedback from teacher and classmates about their 'good bits' and this is recorded on their goal sheets plus their opinions. This is an individual or small group exercise.

Parent information

Students take Parent Information 1 home with their Social Skills folder to discuss with their parents. Remind students to return their folders the following day.

Worksheet 6: STOP the bad habits!

Describe a time when your feelings took over and you used bad habits ... and the problem got worse!

This was the problem at the start

....

....

....

How did you feel?

....

What did you want to happen?

....

....

Then your feelings took over and what happened next?

....

....

....

Could it have worked out better if you had STOPPED first and not let your feelings take over?

....

Parent Information 1: What your child is learning

In STOP THINK DO social skills lessons, the children are currently learning

- To get to know themselves and their classmates better
- To notice positive things and compliment each other
- To pay attention, listen and talk to each other
- To identify and communicate their feelings appropriately
- To control their negative feelings and STOP using bad habits
- To remember the red traffic light and other reminders as cues to STOP.

What can you do to help your child learn these valuable skills?

- When children are learning new skills, it is very helpful for their parents to talk with them about what they are learning
- Parents can also look for and praise any positive changes in their child's behaviour and attitudes
- You may check your child's Social Skills folder and discuss the exercises with them. This folder needs to be returned to school *tomorrow*
- If you would like to discuss this program with your child's teacher, please make an appointment.

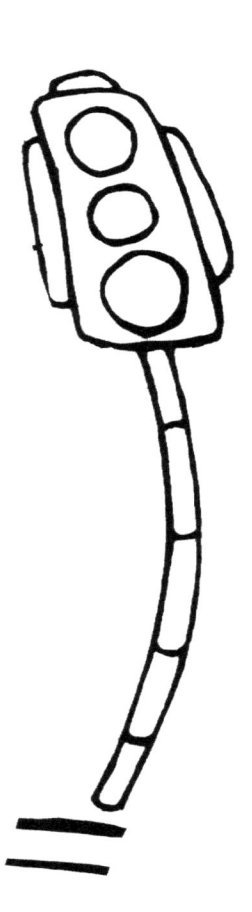

Unit 4: Solving social problems

Aims

- To build on the STOP steps where eyes and ears are used to identify problems and feelings. At THINK, the brain is the key!
- To learn cognitive problem solving skills (brainstorming and consequential thinking) at THINK, signalled by the yellow traffic light
- To understand that social problems are solved by STOPPING and THINKING about options and possible consequences *before* acting
- To learn shorthand terms like Cool, Weak and Aggro, which will help evaluate options and consequences.

Lesson 10: Use your brain

Outcomes
Students learn to:
- experiment with reminders to STOP
- appreciate that their brain loves to THINK
- brainstorm options to solve social problems
- put thinking between feeling and acting

Resources
STOP and THINK posters
Mastercopy 2, pencils, Textas
Worksheet 7
Large sheet of paper or display board
STOP and THINK Friendship video (optional)

Step 1

Exercise: Reminder about reminders

Students complete Worksheet 7. In the circle, discuss the various reminders students have found useful to help them control their feelings and behaviour.

Step 2

Social circle

This lesson we will be talking about what we do after we STOP and control our feelings. Point to the THINK poster. We are at the yellow light, which reminds drivers to get their car into gear ready to go, but not go yet. At THINK, we use our **brains** to think about options and consequences – all the things we could try to solve problems, before we actually do anything. There are millions of ways to solve problems. The more we use our brains to THINK, the smarter we get. Brains love to think!

Step 3

Story/role-play: Using their brains

a. Ask students to imagine this scenario and role-play for impact.

   It is a cold day. Jan has been waiting patiently in the queue to get her lunch. She chats to her cousin Nadia in the other queue. Just as it is her turn to be served, Ethan pushes his way in front of her and begins to order. Jan gets upset and calls him a bad name.

b. Discuss the STOP steps. What is the problem? How are the people feeling?

c. Now to THINK. Point to poster. *What could they try?* Ask children to brainstorm the various options Jan (and Ethan) could try to solve the problem. Record options for display, such as

- She could sulk like she did.
- Or she could abuse Ethan like she did.
- Or she could tell on him to the shop assistant.
- Or she could go to the other queue with her friend. Or …

The aim is to come up with as many options as possible; don't discourage any ideas, no matter how 'silly'. Reinforce students for their 'Good thinking', 'Your brains are hot!' Some suggestions may be role-played.

Alternative resource: Friendship video: Using their brains

a. Show the video from the beginning of Scene 9, p. 49, to the middle of Scene 11, p. 52, where Bonez blocks his ears as Sophie sings. He calls 'Enough!'
b. Recap STOP steps. What is the problem? How are people feeling?
c. Now to THINK. Point to poster. *What could they try?* On a display board or large sheet of paper, list the various options Sophie thinks of to solve the problem with Max. Ask students to brainstorm further suggestions to add to the list, including what Max could do. The aim is to come up with as many options as possible; don't discourage any ideas, no matter how 'silly'. Reinforce students for their 'Good thinking', 'Your brains are hot!' Role-play some of the suggestions.

Step 4

Discussion: Types of options

a. Suggest that the options students brainstormed on the board probably fall into the following categories or types. Write these on the board as well.
   - Stand up for self nicely: ask or speak nicely, compromise, share
   - Ignore: walk away, do something else
   - Get upset: cry, sulk
   - Whinge to an adult
   - Use physical force: hit, grab, push, kick
   - Use verbal abuse: yell, swear, threaten, blame.

b. From the list of options on the board for Jan or Sophie, teacher calls out options one at a time and students identify which category it belongs to from this list. If examples have not been found for some of the categories, ask students to think of more examples to fit.

Step 5

Activity: Personal traffic light poster: THINK

Hand out copies of Mastercopy 2. Students design their own THINK poster (or generate one on the computer) to store in their folder or reduce in size to make a badge or card which may be laminated and worn/carried as a reminder to use their brain and THINK of answers before rushing in to do anything.

Teacher instruction: *Retain list of options for Lessons 11, 12 and 16.*

Worksheet 7: Reminders to STOP

Describe or draw a situation where you had a problem and your reminder worked to STOP your feelings from taking over.

This is what happened first

....

....

This is how I felt

....

But my reminder helped me STOP before my feelings took over, and I did something else instead which worked better.

This is what I did and how it worked out.

....

....

The reminder I am using is (write or draw it)

....

What is the program? 79

Mastercopy 2: THINK poster

Lesson 11: Cool, Weak, Aggro

Outcomes
Students learn to:
- THINK about options in terms of Cool, Weak and Aggro categories
- differentiate Cool, Weak and Aggro options

Resources
THINK poster
Cardboard sheets
Worksheets 8 and 9
Scissors, glue
List of options (from previous lesson)

Step 1

Social circle

a. Refer to the long list of options students thought up to solve Jan's or Sophie's problem last lesson, and the examples of categories or types of options they found. They certainly did plenty of thinking!

b. In this lesson, we describe these categories in shorthand terms like Cool, Weak and Aggro (point to THINK poster) to help us remember them and think of them quickly.

c. Children usually understand Aggro ways, so it is a good place to start.
- Options involving verbal or physical force are examples of the **Aggro** way. Demonstrate a 'clenched fist'.
- Options involving upset emotions or whingeing to adults are examples of the **Weak** way. Demonstrate a 'thumbs down' sign.
- Options involving positive attitudes and behaviours, standing up nicely for yourself or ignoring are examples of the **Cool** way. Demonstrate a 'thumbs up' sign.

Step 2

Activity: Hand signals

a. Distribute a cardboard sheet and Worksheet 8 to each student. They cut the worksheet down the centre, retaining the descriptions of Cool, Weak and Aggro ways. They glue the hand signals on the card and cut them out.

b. Teacher calls out some options from the brainstorm list. Students show the hand signal to match the option. Children will not always agree and need to learn more about the characteristics of Cool, Weak and Aggro.

Step 3

Role-play: Cool, Weak, Aggro

a. Ask students to select an Aggro way from the list of Jan or Sophie's options (for instance, pushing back to the front of queue). Some students role-play this option. The other students describe how the character looks, sounds and feels. Is she standing too close, yelling, pushing and feeling angry? This is the Aggro way. Refer to Worksheet 8 for more characteristics of Aggro.

b. Students then select a Weak option (for instance, whingeing to the salesperson) from the brainstorm list and role-play it. Other students describe how the character looks, sounds and feels. Is she slumping, head down, sighing, crying, feeling miserable and unconfident? This is the Weak way. Refer to Worksheet 8 for more characteristics of Weak.

c. Students then select a Cool option (for instance, ignoring the boy and joining her friend in the next queue) and role-play it. Other students describe how the character looks, sounds and feels. Is she standing straight, head up, staying calm and feeling OK as she decides to do something else? This is the Cool way. Refer to Worksheet 8 for more characteristics of Cool.

d. However, there is no absolute differentiation of these categories. For example, a young child may say that it is Cool to tell an adult if they have a problem, while an older child may think that it is Weak or even Aggro; it all depends on how they feel, look and act when they tell the adult. The main point is for students to be thinking about such categories as short-cut ways to find options, rather than being too precise about the categories.

e. Regarding telling an adult about teasing, stress that children who are being seriously bullied or harassed or frightened need to speak to an adult because they cannot solve this problem themselves; this is not Weak.

Step 4

Exercise: Cool, Weak, Aggro ways

Students complete Worksheet 9. If students aren't sure, instruct them to consider how the person might look, sound and feel, as described on Worksheet 8.

Teacher instruction: *Retain lists of options for Jan or Sophie for next lesson.*

Worksheet 8: Descriptions of Cool, Weak and Aggro ways

The Cool way is to

- Speak in a friendly but firm way
- Stand straight, use eye contact
- Stay calm
- Ignore, compromise
- Feel okay, in control, confident

The Weak way is to

- Mumble
- Look down, slump over
- Give in, cry, sulk, whinge
- Tell on others, dob
- Feel unconfident, upset

The Aggro way is to

- Yell, abuse
- Stand too close, threaten
- Push, hit, kick
- Tease, blame, put down
- Feel angry, out of control

Worksheet 9: Cool, Weak, Aggro ways

Circle the hand signal that matches the option described

Your teacher doesn't choose you for a game so you ...

    Yell at the teacher

    Sulk and begin to cry

    Wait your turn

    Walk off in a huff

    Say you didn't want to play anyway

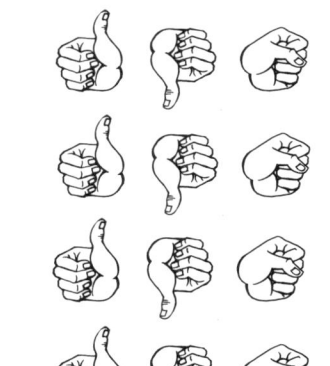

Your friend chooses to play with another group at lunchtime so you ...

    Join in another group's game

    Tell her that she is no longer your friend and cry

    Kick the person your friend is playing with

    Offer the group your ball if they let you play

    Tell the teacher that no one will play with you

You find your lunchbox on the ground so you ...

    Blame the child next to you

    Whinge that it is not fair

    Pick it up and put it back in your bag

    Throw someone else's lunchbox on the ground

Lesson 12: THINK about consequences

> **Outcomes**
> Students learn to:
> - consider possible consequences of options
> - understand that Cool ways often have better consequences
>
> **Resources**
> THINK poster
> Worksheet 10
> List of options (from previous lesson)
> Social problems in Appendix (p. 207) displayed or photocopied
> *STOP and THINK Friendship* video (optional)

Step 1

Social circle

a. Review Cool, Weak or Aggro options for trying to solve problems. Check that students understand these concepts and the characteristics of each.

b. But how do we know which option is the best one? This lesson focuses on using our brains to THINK about the likely consequences of each option. Point to the THINK poster. *What might happen then?* Thinking about consequences will help us decide which to choose.

Step 2

Story/role-play: Consequences!!!

a. Remind students of the story of Jan and the list of Cool, Weak and Aggro options students thought of for resolving the problem with Ethan.

b. Select an Aggro option from the list (for instance, screaming at Ethan).
Ask students
> *'What might happen if she tried that option?'*

Brainstorm possible consequences and record them on the board or paper to retain. These consequences may be role-played in small groups. Ask students how they feel about these consequences
> *'Would you be happy with that outcome?'*

c. Similarly, select a Weak option (for instance, sulking) and then a Cool option (for instance, asking Ethan nicely to wait his turn) from the list. Ask questions as above. Students brainstorm possible consequences which are recorded, and some are role-played. Check how students feel about these consequences.

d. Compare the likely consequences of the Cool, Weak and Aggro ways.
   - Aggro ways generally make people aggro back.
   - Weak ways make people ignore or laugh at them.
   - Cool ways often get friendly reactions and positive consequences.

Alternative resource: Friendship video: Consequences!!!

a. Show the video from the middle of Scene 11, p. 52, from Bonez's comment 'Let's go through some of your options and check out the consequences' to the end of p. 53, after Sophie wins the garden gnome.

b. Select one of Sophie's Aggro options from the list (for instance, screaming at Max). Ask students
   'What might happen if she tried that option?'

   Brainstorm possible consequences and write them on the board or paper to retain. These may be role-played in small groups. Ask students how they feel about these consequences
   'Would you be happy with that outcome?'

c. Similarly, select a Weak option (for instance, crying) and then a Cool option (for instance, making a deal with Max that he can have his turn after her) from the list. Ask students to brainstorm possible consequences, record them and role-play some. Check how students feel about these consequences.

d. Compare the likely consequences of the Cool, Weak and Aggro ways.
   - Aggro ways generally make people aggro back.
   - Weak ways make people ignore or laugh at them.
   - Cool ways often get friendly reactions and positive consequences.

Step 3

Exercise: Options and consequences

a. Hand out Worksheet 10. The list of social problems in the Appendix (p. 207) is photocopied or displayed for students.

b. Students in pairs choose a problem from this list and work together to complete the exercise. With younger children, the teacher may directly instruct throughout the worksheet. Situations may be role-played to help students decide on consequences.

Teacher instruction: Retain
   a. List of social problems from Appendix (p. 207) for next lesson
   b. Lists of options and consequences (Jan/Sophie) for Lesson 16.

Worksheet 10: THINK about options and consequences

STOP

What is the problem? *(Choose one from the list)*

....

How are you feeling about it?

....

How is the other person feeling about it?

....

You have STOPPED to work out what is happening and how people are feeling. Now it's time to use your brain and

THINK

What options can you try to solve this problem?

1. You could ....

Is that Cool, Weak or Aggro? ....

OR

2. You could ....

Is that Cool, Weak or Aggro? ....

What might happen if you try these options?

What might happen if you tried the *first* idea?
This might happen

....

OR this might happen

....

What might happen if you tried the *second* idea?
This might happen

....

OR this might happen

....

Whoa! Your brain is really sizzling!

Unit 5: The cool and friendly way

Aims

- To appreciate that the Cool way generally leads to more acceptable consequences
- To learn the Friendly way – stepping into other people's shoes to see it from their perspective, being fair, considerate, respectful
- To understand that the Friendly way is usually compatible with the Cool way
- To consider many people's feelings and consequences in very tricky problems that involve a moral dilemma
- To learn the Co-operative way to behave when people belong to a group – Co-operative = Cool + Friendly.

Lesson 13: Thumbs up for Cool and Friendly

Outcomes
Students learn to:
> use Cool ways for more acceptable consequences
> consider other people – the Friendly way
> understand that Cool is often Friendly

Resources
STOP and THINK posters
Hand signals (from lesson 11)
Recipe books
Worksheet 11
List of social problems (from previous lesson)
STOP and THINK Friendship video (optional)

Step 1

Social circle

a. Review the likely consequences of using Cool, Weak or Aggro ways to solve social problems.

b. This lesson focuses on Cool ways to behave since they are likely to have better consequences. We will also talk about Friendly ways – stepping into other people's shoes and considering their feelings. Point to poster. Cool and Friendly ways often go together.

Step 2

Discussion: Thumbs up for Cool

a. Ask students to picture the following

You are working in class and another child keeps giggling and talking to you. You ask her to be quiet and the teacher tells you off for talking.

b. Pointing to the posters to guide the STOP and THINK steps, ask students
- What is happening in this story? How would you feel?
- What options could you try to solve the problem? Is each option Cool, Weak or Aggro?
- Students show hand signals to match the options suggested.
- THINK of Cool ways where you stand up for yourself but you remain calm and in control.

- This is also likely to be Friendly to the other person because you are not getting angry or emotional at them and you are behaving respectfully to them. You treat them like you want to be treated.
c. Role-play Cool and Friendly options to this problem in small groups. Other problem situations from the list may be discussed/role-played as above.
d. Brainstorm rules for behaving in Cool and Friendly ways in conflicts, for example
    - Face the other person, give eye contact and stand straight
    - Stay calm and in control
    - Speak in a firm but friendly manner
    - If the person made a mistake, calmly explain what happened
    - Listen to the person's response
    - If you made a mistake, say 'Sorry'
    - Discuss a solution; be prepared to compromise.

Additional resource: Friendship video: Cool and Friendly

a. Replay the short Scene 5, p. 47, where Brent acts Cool to join the game. Ask the students to comment on the verbal, non-verbal and emotional characteristics of Brent's Cool and Friendly way. Replay the clip a number of times to check.
b. Students discuss further Cool and Friendly options Brent or the other children in the story could try to resolve this issue. These may be role-played for practice in Cool and Friendly ways.

Step 3

Activity: Cool and Friendly recipes

a. Introduce the concept of recipes by showing students some recipe books. Point out that there are ingredients and a method to follow to bake a cake.
b. Hand out Worksheet 11. Students form small groups and work together to outline a recipe for Cool and Friendly solutions to one of the problems on the social problem list. Remind them that their brains love THINKING about ways to solve problems, especially Cool and Friendly ways!
c. Each group nominates a spokesperson to present the recipe designed by their group to the class.
d. These recipes may be collected and made into a 'Recipes for Cool and Friendly Solutions' booklet for the classroom and school library.

Worksheet 11: Our recipe for a Cool and Friendly solution

Which problem did you choose for your recipe?

....

....

What Cool and Friendly ingredients do you need?

What voice? ....

What face? ....

What body language? ....

What feelings? ....

How do you put the ingredients together to make a Cool and Friendly cake?

This is what I would do ....

....

....

How does everyone involved feel about this ending to the story?

I feel ....

The other person in the story feels ....

Draw your Cool and Friendly solution below.

Lesson 14: Very tricky moral problems

Outcomes
Students learn to:
- be aware of the pressure friends can put on them
- consider the feelings of people who may not be present
- use their brains in moral dilemmas

Resources
STOP and THINK posters
Worksheet 12

Step 1

Social circle

a. Introduce the concept of very tricky problems when there is a moral issue about right and wrong. In these situations, we need to think about what is good for us (Cool) and what is good for our friend (Friendly).

b. But we also need to think about other people who are not even present at the time. What would our parents, teachers, other adults like police or an important friend feel or say or do if we chose a particular option? We need to consider these consequences as well. Wow, this will test our brains!

Step 2

Discussion: A very tricky moral problem

a. Ask students to close their eyes and imagine the following situation.

Thomas and Rohan were great friends. They enjoyed each other's company and went everywhere together. One day, Thomas decided to get a drink from the local shop, as it was a very hot day. While Thomas was selecting his drink, Rohan moved over to the sweets counter and picked up a box of Smarties and slipped them into his pocket. Thomas paid for his drink and they left the shop. But Thomas had seen his best friend steal the Smarties box.

b. Following the STOP and THINK posters, discuss this situation.
- STOP and find out what actually happened.
- How does Thomas feel?
- How does Rohan feel?
- THINK about what Thomas could do? Is this Cool, Weak or Aggro?
- What could Rohan do? Is this Cool, Weak or Aggro?
- Is it a Friendly thing to do, considering the other person?

c. BUT Thomas and Rohan should consider more people than just each other in this situation. They should think

- Is it a Friendly thing to do to the shop assistant whom they know?
- And what about their parents if they knew?

Our brains will really be smoking with this tricky problem!!

Extension discussion: Staying out of trouble

a. Emphasise that while it is difficult to consider everyone in these tricky problems, using your brains to STOP and THINK about options and consequences is likely to help you stay out of trouble.

b. Behaving in a Friendly way does not necessarily mean that your friend will like your choice of option, especially if you are saying 'No' to them. It does mean that you have considered your friend's position but you may have a different opinion about what is good for them. The same applies to all the people that you have considered when thinking about what to do.

c. Very tricky problems often involve weighing up short- and long-term consequences. What might seem easy or fun or tempting to do at the time might have serious negative results later, for instance, affect your health, get you in trouble with the law, get you suspended from school or cost a lot of money to fix.

d. Various moral dilemmas may be discussed, such as situations involving pressure to set fires, vandalise places, take or sell drugs, lie, cheat. Teachers discuss at a level to suit the students' age and maturity.

Step 3

Exercise: A very tricky problem to solve

Complete Worksheet 12. This may be done as an individual or group activity.

Teacher preparation: *Collect magazines and newspapers for next lesson.*

Worksheet 12: A very tricky problem

STOP

The problem: You didn't learn for the maths test. Emily who sits next to you is good at maths. You try to copy her work.

The feelings: You are worried about failing. Emily looks embarrassed and annoyed at you.

THINK

What could you do?
Keep cheating

Is that Cool, Weak or Aggro? ....

Is it Friendly to Emily? ....

What might happen if you did this?

I might pass the test

BUT Emily might ....

AND there are others to consider too ...

What might your teacher think and do if he or she knew?

....

What might your friends say and do if they knew you were a cheat?

....

What might your mother think and do if she knew?

....

....

Can you think of a Cool way to feel okay yourself
AND still consider Emily's feelings in a Friendly way
AND also consider your teacher, your mother and your friends?

....

....

What a tricky problem!

Lesson 15: Co-operative = Cool + Friendly

Outcomes
Students learn to:
- understand that we all belong to groups
- value groups functioning well
- use co-operative ways in groups (i.e. Cool + Friendly ways)

Resources
A piece of string (about 50 cm long) per student, strings divided into five piles, each pile rolled into a ball
Glue, large sheets of paper
Textas, pencils
Magazine, scissors
Parent Information 2

Step 1

Social circle

a. What do students understand by the word *co-operation*? List their ideas on the board.
b. This lesson looks at Cool and Friendly ways for co-operating in groups.

Step 2

Activity: A team effort

a. Organise the class into 5 teams of students seated in circles. One student from each group is given a ball of string. This student begins a story while unwinding a piece of string for example,

   Once upon a time there was a ....

   As soon a student unwinds his or her piece of string, they stop the story and pass the ball on to the next student.

b. Students continue to pass the ball around the circle, each unwinding a piece of string and adding to the story until their piece of string is unwound from the ball. A group story is thus generated by the team effort. Each of the five teams will have different stories and some teams will work better than others.

Step 3

Discussion: Co-operative = Cool + Friendly

a. Return to the social circle. Discuss how the group stories evolved. Identify factors that helped the story progress well and those that messed it up.
b. For groups to work well, the people in the group cannot always have their own way or there would be constant hassles and nothing would get done. They also have to consider other people's feelings and views. This means a combination of Cool and Friendly behaviour. This is the Co-operative way in groups. When our teams used these techniques, the task of creating a group story went well.

Step 4

Group activity: A community groups collage

a. Brainstorm types of groups that students know about or belong to. Students also think about the rules that these groups have, to guide their members to cooperate, like the rules we use for our social skills lessons.
b. Students divide into small groups to find and cut out pictures in magazines where people belong to particular groups. Each small group of students finds pictures relevant to a particular community group, for instance, sporting, social, family, school, musical or religious group.
c. Students stick their pictures on large sheets of paper or a display board under the relevant headings such as Sport, School, Social, Family, Religious, etc., to make up a collage about groups. Even this activity is a team effort requiring Cool + Friendly behaviour!

Alternative group activity: Co-operation Rules!

Students design a large poster for the class entitled 'Co-operation *Rules!*' where they list the most important rules for a successful group. For example
- Everyone has a chance to speak and give their ideas
- Say your ideas in a Cool way
- Others should listen: ask them politely to listen if they are distracted
- Treat others like you want to be treated – the Friendly way
- If there is disagreement, STOP and THINK to solve the problem by discussing options and consequences as a group
- If the group is working on a task, each member should understand what they need to do and when.

Parent information

Distribute Parent Information 2 for students to take home with their Social Skills folder to discuss with their parents. Remind them to return folders the next day.

Parent Information 2: What your child is learning

STOP THINK DO social skills lessons, the children are currently learning

- To think of many ways to solve problems with other people
  Some are Cool, some are Weak, some are Aggro ways
- To try Cool ways because they have better consequences
  Cool means standing up for yourself in a positive way
- Cool ways are usually Friendly
  Friendly means considering other people's feelings and views
- To use Co-operative ways in groups so that they function well
  Co-operative means Cool + Friendly
- To remember the yellow traffic light as a cue to THINK.

What can you do to help your child learn these valuable skills?

- When children are learning new skills, it is very helpful for their parents to talk with them about what they are learning.
- Parents can also look for and praise any positive changes in their child's behaviour and attitudes.
- You may check your child's Social Skills folder and discuss the exercises with your child. This folder needs to be returned to school *tomorrow*.
- If you would like to discuss this program with your child's teacher, please make an appointment.

UNIT 6: DOING IT!

Aims

- To choose options that have the best likely consequences at DO, as signalled by the green traffic light
- To learn behavioural skills for putting chosen options into practice
- To get students' bodies into shape so they send the right signals to others
- To practise skills for making and keeping friends.

Lesson 16: Fine-tune your body

Outcomes
Students learn to:
  choose options with the best consequences
  put chosen options into action using voice, facial and distance cues

Resources
STOP THINK and DO posters
Mastercopy 3, pencils, Textas
List of options/consequences (from lesson 12)
Worksheet 13
STOP and THINK Friendship video (optional)

Step 1

Social circle

a) Sing the STOP THINK DO song or Three Bright Lights.
b) We have learnt how to STOP and THINK about ways of behaving. We are up to DO. Point to the DO poster. The green light is on. It tells the car driver to go and it tells us to DO something to solve problems. We have to get our body right so we DO it right.

Step 2

Story/role-play: Fine-tuning her body

a. Refer to the lists of options and consequences discussed for Jan in earlier lessons. Point to DO poster. *What is the best option?* After weighing up the consequences of various options, students choose the best one, that is, the one with the most acceptable consequences. A majority vote may be taken to decide which option to DO. This is likely to be a Cool option (such as asking Ethan nicely to wait his turn).

b. But to solve the problem effectively, Jan must do it properly so she sends the right signals to Ethan. *How would she do it?* Point to poster. She has to fine-tune her body in terms of her
   - facial expressions
   - voice tone and volume
   - distance she stands from him.

c. Students role-play this option a number of times using the same words (for instance, 'Excuse me, Ethan, but it was my turn first') BUT varying voice, face and distance. In different role-plays, Jan alters
   - the facial cues – sulks or glares or frowns
   - the voice cues – whispers or yells or speaks very quickly
   - the distance cues – stands too close or too far away or sits down.

d. After each variation, students discuss how the actor playing Ethan in the role-play feels and how he would respond if someone gave him this signal. Would it solve the original problem or could it make it worse?

Alternative resource: Friendship video: Fine-tuning her body

a. Show the video from beginning of p. 54 in script (after Bonez congratulated Sophie on being a winner) to the end of Scene 12, p. 56.
b. After weighing up the consequences of various options, Sophie finally chose a Cool option of asking Max nicely to wait his turn. She must do this option properly so she sends the right signals to Max. And it worked!
c. BUT, let's imagine that she gave Max the wrong signals with her voice or face or distance cues. Students role-play Scene 12 a number of times, each time varying face, voice or distance while still using the *same* words as Sophie uses in the script. In different role-plays, Sophie alters
    - the distance cues – stands too close or too far away or sits down
    - the voice cues – whispers or yells or speaks very quickly
    - the facial cues – sulks or glares or frowns.
d. After each variation, discuss how the actor playing Max feels and how he would respond if someone gave him this signal. Could it make it worse?

Step 3

Exercise: Doing it well

a. Hand out Worksheet 13. Read out the problem and instruct students to imagine the scenario. It may also be role-played. If the *STOP and THINK Friendship* video is available, show Scene 14, p. 57, where this scenario is repeated twice to reinforce details.
b. Students form groups of three. One child has the role of Noni, another is Brent and the third is Wendy. Each member of the group gives their feelings and options in their role and records them on the worksheet. They discuss possible consequences of these options as a group.
c. At DO, each group chooses their best option. If they do not all agree, they find an acceptable compromise that they will all try, or they vote on options and go with the majority. In the groups of three, they then decide how to put their chosen option into action in terms of the face, voice and distance they will use when they role-play it for the class next lesson.

Step 4

Activity: Personal traffic light poster: DO

Hand out copies of Mastercopy 3. Students design their DO poster (or generate one on the computer) to store in their folder or reduce in size to make a badge or card which may be laminated and worn/carried as a reminder to DO it well!

Worksheet 13: Doing it well

STOP

What is the problem?
Children are playing basketball. Noni misses the ball and is teased by others, especially Wendy. Brent tries to support her.

What are the feelings?
How does Noni feel? ....

How does Wendy feel? ....

How does Brent feel? ....

THINK

What options could they try?

Noni could ....

OR she could ....

Wendy could ....

OR she could ....

Brent could ....

OR he could ....

Discuss the consequences of these options.

DO

Choose the option your group thinks is best
If you don't agree, find a compromise; one you will all agree to try.

....

Is this Cool and Friendly?..

How would they actually DO it?

How would their voices sound?

....

How would their faces look?

....

Where would they stand?

....

Be ready to role-play your chosen DO with your group.

What is the program? | 101

Mastercopy 3: DO poster

Lesson 17: What friends do

Outcomes
Students learn to:
- identify skills needed to make and keep friends
- identify 'good bits' about friends
- use STOP THINK DO to solve problems with friends

Resources
STOP THINK DO posters
Worksheet 13 (previous lesson)
Worksheets 14 and 15
Paper, pencils

Step 1

Social circle

a. Students bring their worksheets from the previous lesson to the circle. Each group of three role-plays its chosen option at DO, sending the right signals in terms of facial expressions, distance and voice to solve the problem.

b. Teacher reinforces students' efforts and shapes their behaviour with guiding comments if they are not quite conveying the right message. Invite students to comment on the role-plays like film directors, offering ideas on voice, face and body cues. While they are role-playing, children may change their minds about their choice of DO or how they DO it because of feedback they receive. This is why practise in groups is so useful!

c. Emphasise that, as with any skill (riding bicycles, spelling, football), we can't always get it right the first time we try social skills either. We need to get our body into shape and this means practice. And practising our skills in lessons helps us get it right in real life!

d. Fine-tuning our bodies so we get it right is just what we need to make and keep friends. Discuss how important friends are throughout our lives. In this lesson we will learn more about what to DO to make and keep friends, and how to DO it!

Step 2

Discussion: Making and keeping friends

a. Remember how we got to know each other better in our early lessons? Ask students to recall rules for meeting and getting to know people, since these are the same rules for making friends initially. For example
- Say 'Hello' nicely
- Get eye contact

- Ask questions about the other person to show we are interested
- Listen to their answers, pay attention
- Find things we like that are similar
- Be positive.

b. What extra skills do we need to keep friends once we have made them? Students brainstorm 'What is a friend?' with the group. On the board, draw up a list of things friends DO for and with each other, and what friends DON'T do to each other, for example

- Spend time with them
- Listen to their point of view even if you don't agree
- Accept them even if they make mistakes
- Say and do friendly things for them
- Don't push them around
- Try and help them if they have a problem
- Share and co-operate with them
- Bargain and compromise with them so you both win
- Behave in a Cool and Friendly way with them
- Stand up for yourself but consider their feelings too.

Step 3

Exercise: Handling rejection from a friend

a. Discuss with students how they feel when their friends DON'T do friendly things to or for them. How do they handle rejection by their friends?
b. Fortunately, when friends have problems with each other, they can follow the STOP THINK DO steps to solve it in Cool and Friendly ways. In pairs, students complete Worksheet 14, following the traffic light posters.

Step 4

Activity: Friendship collage

Using Worksheet 15, students make a collage of drawings or descriptions of all their friends around them. They can include peers, family members, pets, teachers past and present, neighbours, pen pal, Scout group, teddy, and so on.

Alternative activity: 'Wanted' friend poster

Students design a 'Wanted' poster about a friend. They draw a picture of a friend at the top of the page and then describe them in terms of the things that make them special or the things they like about them, for instance, what their friend looks like, what games they play, what they don't like doing, how they help you, what they are good at. These posters may be displayed around the room.

Worksheet 14: Handling rejection from a friend

STOP

The problem
Your friend ignores you and plays with someone else. You don't know why.

The feelings

You felt ....

Your friend seemed to feel ....

THINK

What could you try?

1. ....

Is this Cool, Weak or Aggro? ....

2. ....

Is this Cool, Weak or Aggro? ....

What might happen if you try these options?

1. ....

2. ....

DO

What would you choose to do?

....

Is it Cool and Friendly? ....

How would you actually DO it?

How would your face look? Draw it.

....

How would your voice sound?

....

Where would you stand?

....

Don't forget to use STOP THINK DO next time with your friend.

Worksheet 15: My friends with me

Me

Unit 7: Dealing with Unfriendly Behaviour

Aims

- To recognise negative pressure, teasing, put-downs and physical bullying from others
- To develop emotional control, cognitive and behavioural skills to deal with negative behaviour and pressure from others
- To identify support systems around children when they feel unable to handle negative pressure alone.

Lesson 18: Saying 'No'

Outcomes
Students learn to:
> practise saying 'no' to negative pressure using face, voice and distance cues
> recognise put-downs and teasing

Resources
Large sheet of paper or display board
Worksheet 16
STOP and THINK Friendship video (optional)

Step 1

Social circle

Teacher writes a big 'NO' on the board. Ask students to give examples of times when they do or should say 'No' to their friends, if they don't agree with their actions, comments or requests that might seem unfair or unreasonable.

Step 2

Role-play: Saying 'No' the Cool way

a. Hand out Worksheet 16 to students, who work in pairs facing each other in the social circle to role-play the situations described.
b. As a group, discuss the rules for saying 'No' the Cool way
   - Get eye contact with the person
   - Use a serious face and voice, as if you mean it
   - You don't have to give reasons, but you can
   - If they keep pressuring you or threaten you, say 'No' again and walk away; they are certainly not behaving in a Friendly way
   - If they follow you and keep pressuring you, tell an adult.

Step 3

Discussion: Teasing

Ask students to brainstorm examples of put-downs and teasing. Suggest that people who put down and tease
   - Hurt someone's feelings
   - Have power over someone
   - Keep it secret to avoid trouble
   - Do it repeatedly to wear the person down
   - Create a victim.

Alternative resource: *Friendship* video: Teasing

a. Replay Scene 14, p. 57, showing examples of teasing and put-downs (or students may use the script to role-play the incident themselves).
b. What words describe what is happening to Noni? What are put-downs and teasing? Brainstorm ideas. People who put down and tease
   - Hurt someone's feelings
   - Have power over someone
   - Keep it secret to avoid trouble
   - Do it repeatedly to wear the person down
   - Create a victim.

Step 4

Activity: Group anti-teasing tricks

Introduce the idea that there are Cool techniques to handle teasing. On the board or on paper to retain, draw three columns as shown below.

STOP	THINK	DO
The problem	What could you try?	**Anti-teasing tricks that work!**
The feelings	What might happen then?	

a. Point to the STOP column. Students give examples of teasing they have experienced or witnessed, without mentioning names to blame anyone. Write examples under 'The problem'.
b. Taking one example of teasing, ask students how they would feel if they were teased like that. Record answers under 'The feelings'. It is useful for children to hear that not everyone feels the same about teasing.
c. Point to the THINK column. Students think what they could do if they were teased like that. Record options and discuss possible consequences.
d. In the DO column, children volunteer ideas that have worked for them. Leave list displayed and provide opportunities to add more anti-teasing tricks to it before next lesson.

Teacher note: *The STOP THINK DO process outlined 'de-emotionalises' issues like teasing and reframes them as problem-solving exercises for students. This process may be applied to many problems affecting the group, for instance, distracting behaviour.*

Worksheet 16: Saying 'No' the Cool way

You and your partner choose who will be student 1 and student 2 first.

Student 1:   'I like your hat. Give it to me … I want to wear it.'

Student 2:   Look at student 1 and say in a calm, firm voice,
'No, you can't wear my hat today.'

Student 1:   'Let's smash the windows in the toilets.'

Student 2:   Look at student 1 and say in a calm, firm voice
'No, I don't think it's right to smash things.'

Student 1:   'I saw money in your bag. I need to borrow some for the canteen. I'll pay you back later.'

Student 2:   Look at student 1 and say in a calm, firm voice,
'No, I need the money for my own lunch.'

Now student 1 and 2 switch roles

Student 1:   'Come for a swim with us. Who cares if you're a bit late home?'

Student 2:   Look at student 1 and say in a calm, firm voice,
'No, I have to go home after soccer.'

Student 1:   'Look at Shannon; he's such a pain. Let's hassle him for fun.'

Student 2:   Look at student 1 and say in a calm, firm voice,
'No, I don't want to hassle Shannon.'

Student 1:   'Let's take your sister's make up and play with it.'

Student 2:   Look at student 1 and say in a calm, firm voice
'No, I wouldn't like my things treated like that.'

Lesson 19: Teasing and bullying

Outcomes
Students learn to:
- recognise teasing and bullying
- use STOP THINK DO for handling it
- identify people who can assist them

Resources
Anti-teasing tricks (from previous lesson)
Newspapers, magazines
Paper, pencils, Textas
STOP and THINK Friendship workbook (optional)

Step 1

Social circle

a. Review the STOP THINK DO list of teasing problems, feelings, options and cool tricks that work. Discuss new tricks added since last lesson. More ideas are located on p. 36 of the video workbook.

b. Suggest students try tricks from the anti-teasing list when they are teased until they find some that work for them. Suggest they use reminders to remember to use their cool tricks rather than their old habits that did not work, for example, wearing or carrying something special.

c. Students plan how to make their anti-teasing tricks into a booklet for distribution to other classes and use by peer mediators as a reference when they are assisting children to deal with teasing in the yard.

d. In summary, Cool ways of handling teasing generally involve
   - Stay calm, think of something nice, count to ten, sing in your head
   - Ignore, walk away, show it doesn't affect you
   - Do something the teaser doesn't expect like laugh, make a joke, agree with them or say 'Pardon, I didn't hear you'
   - Use your anti-teasing shield described below to block the words.

Step 2

Activity: Anti-teasing shield

a. This is an interesting anti-teasing trick for children of this age. Instruct students to close their eyes and reach out in front of them. Describe that everyone has a force-field of energy around them; it's called our personal space. Instruct them to try to 'feel' it and 'see' it in their mind. Some children will be able to see things like colours or flashing lights and some may feel the tingling in their fingertips.

b. Suggest that when students are teased, they picture their shield in terms of its colour and feel, and then imagine the teasing words bouncing off the shield back to the teaser, so the words can't hurt their feelings.

c. To reinforce the image, students draw their teasing shield in great detail so that they can picture it quickly if they need to use it. Offer some ideas
- What colour is it?
- What shape and size is it?
- Does it have a filter for nice words?
- Does it have lasers to send teasing words back to the teaser?

Step 3

Activity: You are not alone

a. As a group, discuss options students have if their anti-teasing tricks don't work in a situation and they become very upset, or if someone is really physically bullying and frightening them. This might occur anywhere. Discuss examples of bullying that students have experienced or witnessed at school, home, sport, or in the street.

b. Teacher (or students in small groups) finds and reads out articles in newspapers and magazines where someone is being bullied, teased, harassed or put down. Read outcomes of these stories to students to indicate the negative consequences experienced by those who do these very unfriendly things.

c. Students need to understand that it is a universal problem and doesn't just occur to them, and that there are consequences in our society for the perpetrators. They need to be reassured that they are not expected to handle more severe harassment problems alone.

d. Identify 'safe places' and 'safe people' around the school and neighbourhood for students to go to if necessary. Particularly, outline the process children follow in your school to get help.

Lesson 20: We can STOP THINK DO! Yahoo!

Outcomes
Students learn to:
- use cooperative skills to organise a class party
- set tasks and follow through with plans
- review their progress
- celebrate!

Resources
Worksheet 2 (second review)
Pencils, Textas
Co-operation Rules! poster (optional, from Lesson 15)
Worksheet 17
Parent Information 3
STOP and THINK Friendship video (optional); p. 38 of workbook (optional)

Step 1

Social circle

a. We have all learnt so much about social skills since we began the STOP THINK DO lessons. What have we learnt? Review skills for STOP (using eyes and ears to work out feelings and problems), THINK (using brains to solve problems) and DO (fine-tuning bodies to send the right signals).

b. What have we learnt about each other? Remind students of the 'good bits' that have been identified by teacher and classmates. We learned that we can work very well together as a group using STOP THINK DO.

Step 2

Exercise: Have I improved?

Students refer to Worksheet 2 for a review of their progress towards achieving the goals set in Lesson 4. They record positive comments that have been made about them by others, and their opinions. They may set further goals to achieve.

Step 3

Activity: Graduation certificate

Students design their own graduation certificates with computer or pencils, to be formally presented at the party. Alternatively, certificates from p. 38 of the video workbook may be coloured by students.

Additional resource: *Friendship* video: Party time!

Show the party, Scene 17, p. 58. Yes, even Bonez makes mistakes and forgets to use STOP THINK DO sometimes! The students will also make mistakes and go back to their old habits sometimes. But, if they use reminders and keep cool, they will get it right more often. They will get on better with others and feel better about themselves. STOP THINK DO is a good habit they can use all of their life! And, now that they have graduated, they could take over Bonez's job in the Friendship Neighbourhood!

Step 4

Activity: Planning our party!

a. Now it is time to plan our party! Remember our Co-operation *Rules!* poster, using Cool and Friendly ways to work in groups? We will need to use these skills to work together and plan our party. If poster is not available, remind students of the rules for co-operation, that is, Cool + Friendly behaviour.

b. First we identify the tasks that will need to be done for the party to be a success. Teacher offers suggestions as students brainstorm ideas, such as
   - What is the date of the party?
   - Where will we have it?
   - Who will we invite?
   - Will our parents come to the party?
   - Who will design the invitations?
   - What will we eat?
   - What music will we have?
   - What decorations shall we have?
   - Who will take the photos?
   - Who will clean up?

c. Hand out Worksheet 17. Divide the class into groups of four. Assign a different task to each group. Discuss a timeline and a review date to keep them on track. Each group completes the worksheet to clarify their task.

d. The school principal may be invited to the party to officially hand out certificates to students. The successful completion of the program and the final celebration may be reported in the school newsletter and local paper.

Teacher note: *The model of a co-operative group plan on Worksheet 17 may be used in many situations where the class needs to work together on a group task, including a co-operative learning task.*

Parent information

Distribute Parent Information 3 for students to take home to their parents with a note about the party, along with their Social Skills folders for parent feedback.

What is the program? | 115

Worksheet 17: Planning our party!

Use STOP THINK DO to help you work in your small group on the big task of planning our class graduation party.

STOP — **What is the task your small group has in planning our class party?**

....

How do you feel about this task?

....

THINK — **What things does your group have to do to complete their task?**

1. ....

Who will do it?..

2. ....

Who will do it?..

3. ....

Who will do it?..

DO — **Do these things until your group's task is completed by the set date, which is**

....

Then we can all enjoy the party!

Parent Information 3: What your child is learning

In STOP THINK DO social skills lessons, the children are currently learning

- To choose to behave in ways that have the best consequences
- To practise behavioural skills that send the right signals to others
- To remember the green traffic light as a cue to DO these skills
- To make and keep friends
- To handle negative pressure, put downs, teasing and bullying
- To identify support systems around them if they need help
- To co-operate as a class on projects like planning a graduation party.

What can you do to help your child learn these valuable skills?

- When children are learning new skills, it is very helpful for their parents to talk with them about what they are learning.
- Parents can also look for and praise any positive changes in their child's behaviour and attitudes.
- You may check your child's Social Skills folder and discuss the exercises with your child. This folder needs to be returned to school for review purposes.

Since the formal social skills lessons are now finished, your child has graduated from the program and will participate in a class party on

....

We are asking for your help to make the party a success by providing

....

....

Part 4 What is the program?

Part 4 What is the program?

Social skills program for ages 10–12 years

- Overview of the program   118
- Outline of lesson content   119
- Resources used in the program   121
- Lessons for ages 10–12   123

Overview of the program

Suitability of students

STOP THINK DO is suitable for children of all ages and all personalities, including shy, anxious, unconfident, unassertive or immature children, and hyperactive, impulsive, aggressive, bossy children, and all those in between. The program presented in this section of the manual is suitable for children in primary school classrooms in Australian terminology, aged 10–12 years.

The program may be implemented flexibly to suit the needs of students and teachers. The length of the program and the rate of progress through it may be varied according to the location and the age, intelligence or special needs of the children involved. For example, younger students, slower learners, those with hearing or language difficulties or autism, or students from different cultural backgrounds, may require more individual attention, repetition, structure or cueing, with the traffic lights and hand signals being adaptable and powerful visual cues. Students with visual difficulties may follow the language cues with tactile representations of the traffic lights and hand signals.

Assessment

Before the commencement of the classroom program, Student and Teacher Pre-Assessment forms in the Appendix (pp. 208–209) may be completed
- To determine the social strengths and weaknesses of the students
- To provide a baseline for measuring progress from the program.

Post-Assessment forms (pp. 210–211) may be administered immediately following the program and/or later for review.

Lesson format

- A requirement for implementing the program in any context is that the sequential order of the lessons be followed through the STOP, THINK and DO steps.
- While the program lists 20 lessons, it is entirely flexible in terms of the number of lessons or duration of lessons. This is decided by teachers to suit their group.
- Each lesson contains
    - the specific aims of the lesson and materials required
    - a brief review of the previous lesson's concepts or skills
    - the structured teaching of a new core concept or skill
    - a related activity, such as a game, role-play, written exercise, discussion or video
    - an alternative activity or exercise for older children in the age block or those already familiar with the core concept or skill.
- Exercises or other work related to social skills lessons are stored in Social Skills folders made up by students before the program starts, to give it curriculum validity.
- At the completion of each of the STOP, THINK and DO sections, an information sheet is provided for parents.

Outline of lesson content

STOP units

Units 1, 2 and 3 focus on STOP, the hardest step of all, signalled by the red light. The main skills taught at STOP are self-control and perceptual skills. Children are taught

- To hold back so they don't react emotionally and use bad habits
- To use their **eyes and ears** to work out the problem and the feelings people have.

These units also contain group-building activities to promote a cohesive, positive group culture which motivates students to learn and use social skills, and particularly to put in the effort to STOP their old habits and control their emotions.

THINK units

Units 4 and 5 focus on THINK, signalled by the yellow light. The main skills taught at THINK are cognitive problem solving and consequential thinking, so students

- Use their **brains** to think about possible options to try with others
- Evaluate possible consequences of these options.

While the emphasis is on teaching children *how*, not *what* to think, they learn that some options have better consequences and are worth trying. To identify and describe options quickly, they learn shorthand terms: Cool, Weak, Aggro, Friendly and Co-operative ways.

DO units

Units 6 and 7 focus on DO, signalled by the green light. The main skills at this step are decision/choice-making and behavioural skills. Students learn

- To choose the option with the best consequences
- To act on it, fine-tuning the **body** to send the right signals.

The behavioural techniques used to teach these skills in the lessons include modelling, shaping and role-play.

Techniques for developing pro-social motivation

Techniques for motivating children to learn and then apply the STOP THINK DO skills and problem-solving process are built into the program in various ways.

- Activities and exercises to promote group cohesion, the idea that 'we are all in this together', 'we all want to use our new skills' and 'we help each other'.
- Students identify and set goals for themselves and others, monitor progress towards goal achievement, and reinforce achievement in themselves and others.
- Emphasis is placed on the positive aspects of all people in the class, their **'good bits'**. This often represents a reversal of focus within class groups where

'students with problems' or 'problem students' are well known and often receive negative attention. Students drop this habit as they begin to identify with the pro-social group goals.

- There is formal and regular reinforcement of the 'good bits' of all group members, through activities like posting positive messages to designated classmates (such activities may be incorporated into social skills lessons or used at other times).
- A time is set for daily class meetings, say 15 minutes after the lunch break. Children and teachers sit in a 'social circle', which visibly reinforces the group culture. This is a time for informally acknowledging progress in students, doing a formal 'good bits' activity, planning group projects, or for solving problems that affect the group (such as teasing or bullying) using STOP THINK DO. Even after the completion of the formal training program, the social circle may be continued.
- The fact that teachers use STOP THINK DO to manage problems they experience with students motivates students to have confidence in and use the process.
- Students are encouraged to talk to their parents about what they are learning and parents are encouraged to reinforce these new skills and attitudes in the home. Children are more motivated to learn and apply new skills if they feel that these are valued by their parents. Parents also recognise the validity and credibility of the program through its methodological approach and curriculum style of presentation.

Resources used in the program

Traffic light posters

The three posters accompanying the manual illustrate the STOP THINK DO steps. They are introduced separately as the lessons progress and are designed to be displayed vertically (red light on top, yellow below, green on bottom), reflecting an actual traffic light. Students also make personal traffic light posters which may be used in a variety of ways eg. reduced in size and worn as a badge or carried as a reminder.

Stories/role-plays

Social stories and role-playing are essential ingredients of social skills training programs. In the school setting, they provide a relatively inexpensive yet meaningful resource for training myriad skills in students, such as

- Paying attention and remembering details
- Looking and listening carefully
- Being aware of individual differences in people's attitudes and behavioural styles
- Having self-awareness about how others see them
- Identifying and communicating feelings
- Identifying causes for feelings and, therefore, behaviour
- Perspective taking and empathising with others
- Identifying problems and ways to solve them
- Assuming various roles, including ones they may not take in real life
- Practising and fine-tuning skills
- Providing helpful feedback to others
- Co-operation in groups.

All these skills are fundamental to the STOP THINK DO program. In several lessons, students are presented with descriptions of typical social situations and characters with which children of similar age and circumstance can identify. Additional social problem stories are contained in the Appendix (p. 207) for use in lessons or for spontaneous practice and review of concepts and skills at any time. Students can fill out a storyline by brainstorming ideas and/or writing scripts and dialogue for it.

Teachers are urged to present these stories to students in a convincing manner so they can visualise the situation, clarify the issues involved and identify and empathise with the characters. Following the presentation of the story, teachers engage students in structured discussions. Role-plays are devised by teacher and students to provide more impact and also opportunities for skills practice and feedback in a safe environment.

Some students may initially be reluctant to participate in role-plays. However, because the teacher is also utilising motivational techniques throughout the training program to develop a positive group culture, they will soon realise that it is safe and, indeed, rewarding for them to be an active participant in role-playing. Some students may only volunteer for particular roles with which they can identify. However, here is an ideal opportunity for teachers to assign students roles that they are unlikely to assume in real life, ensuring more varied practice and modelling opportunities, which will broaden their skills base.

An alternative option to storytelling that utilises the visual medium for impact is for teachers to tape suitable social scenarios from television programs popular with their students and to present these, following them up with student discussion and role-play, again pursuing the structure recommended in the program.

STOP and THINK Friendship video package

The *STOP and THINK Friendship* video package is an *optional* resource, which does not accompany this manual and is not essential to the programs in this manual. In several lessons, teachers have the option of using storytelling or a relevant clip from the *Friendship* video for discussion and role-play. However, while it is not essential, the program is greatly enhanced by the *Friendship* video, which was developed specifically to use an appealing visual medium to demonstrate the STOP THINK DO steps to children in a powerful way.

The video package contains

- Real-life scenarios of social problem situations with which children of primary-school age can identify immediately
- A humorous set, the Friendship Neighbourhood, where resides Bonez, a young adolescent who guides the characters in the video (and the viewers) through the STOP THINK DO steps for making and keeping friends. Bonez has credibility as a mentor and mediator, since he once had problems but was helped by STOP THINK DO
- A demonstration of techniques to use *and* those to avoid when relating with peers
- A combination of powerful teaching techniques; direct instruction by Bonez in the STOP THINK DO steps plus modelling of skills by the children in the video clips
- Exercises on a CD-ROM and a workbook for photocopying included in the video package, which can extend those in this training manual
- The full video script in the workbook where teachers can identify the exact clips for lessons as cited in this manual, and also as cues for role-playing exercises.

Other STOP THINK DO resources

In the Appendix is a list of all STOP THINK DO resources (p. 213) that complement the programs in this manual. Some have been mentioned earlier in this book.

Lessons for ages 10-12

STOP

Unit 1:	**Getting to know people**	**125**
	Lesson 1: Getting to know you and me	126
	Lesson 2: Similarities and differences	129
	Lesson 3: All eyes and ears	131
Unit 2:	**Look and listen for feelings**	**133**
	Lesson 4: Liking me, liking you	134
	Lesson 5: Identifying feelings	137
	Lesson 6: Reasons for feelings	141
Unit 3:	**Communicating feelings**	**145**
	Lesson 7: Being positive	146
	Lesson 8: STOP the bad habits	149
	Lesson 9: Reminders to STOP	152
	Parent information 1	155

THINK

Unit 4:	**Solving social problems**	**157**
	Lesson 10: Use your brain	158
	Lesson 11: Cool, Weak, Aggro	161
	Lesson 12: THINK about consequences	165
Unit 5:	**The cool and friendly way**	**169**
	Lesson 13: Thumbs up for Cool and Friendly	170
	Lesson 14: Very tricky moral problems	173
	Lesson 15: Co-operative = Cool + Friendly	176
	Parent information 2	178

DO

Unit 6:	**DOing it!**	**179**
	Lesson 16: Fine-tune your body	180
	Lesson 17: What friends DO	185
Unit 7:	**Dealing with unfriendly behaviour**	**189**
	Lesson 18: Saying 'No'	190
	Lesson 19: Teasing and bullying	192
	Lesson 20: We can STOP THINK DO! Yahoo!	194
	Parent information 3	197

Unit 1: Getting to know people

Aims

- To learn skills for meeting and talking to people
- To introduce and reinforce rules for behaviour in lessons
- To learn more about each other, the similarities and differences
- To increase children's awareness of themselves and how they appear to others
- To encourage positive communication and interaction between students and develop a supportive group environment/culture in the classroom.

Lesson 1: Getting to know you and me

Outcomes
Students learn to:
> negotiate rules and consequences for behaviour
> understand more about themselves and others
> use listening, observing and questioning skills
> learn rules for meeting and talking to people

Resources
Poster for group rules
Name tags for each student on Mastercopy 1 (plus extra)
Pins

Step 1

Social circle

a. Sit with students in a circle and explain the following:
   We are going to spend some time this term learning how to get on better with each other and make our classroom and our playground an even happier place to learn and play. We will have lessons called STOP THINK DO. You may already be familiar with the program and this will be an extension of what you have learnt. We will usually begin lessons with a social circle like this.

b. Introduce rules for social skills lessons. Discuss why we need rules in any group – so everyone has a fair go and a chance to learn and participate. Invite suggestions for rules for our circle, and about what will happen when we keep and break the rules. Encourage all students to contribute ideas for suitable management strategies and to take responsibility for reminding others about the rules and consequences. Encourage and reward those who follow the rules throughout the lessons.

c. Students decide on rules and record them on a poster displayed throughout the lessons. Rules may include
   - We listen to each other
   - Everyone has a turn to speak
   - Everyone can join in
   - We do not put others down.

Step 2

Activity: Pay attention!

a. Choose two students. Student 1 initiates a conversation with student 2 about the sports or swimming carnival, and their achievements on the day. Before the conversation begins, teacher takes student 2 aside and instructs them to listen carefully, be attentive and enjoy what is being said.

b. Repeat the exercise with the same topic. This time, instruct student 2 to pay very little attention, look away from student 1, fidget, find interest in something else near them, chat to someone else.

c. Ask the group to identify what is happening in both role-plays. Identify the differences in the body language, voice, facial expressions and involvement of student 2.

d. Discuss broader implications of this activity in terms of rules for meeting and getting to know people generally. How do we approach people we don't know? What do we typically say to engage people in conversation? How do we behave when we are talking? Rules may include
   - Approach them, smile, say 'Hello' and introduce yourself
   - Ask questions about them
   - Listen carefully to their answers, pay attention
   - Discuss things you have in common or could do together.

Step 3

Game: Listen ... who am I?

a. Have you noticed that when the topic of conversation is important to you, you tend to take more notice and listen carefully? Since listening is such an important skill in finding out more about other people and ourselves, let's have some practice with something that might interest you.

b. Line the class up along a wall facing away from you. Pin a name tag from Mastercopy 1 (plus extra tags of locally relevant character names if needed) on the back of each student. Announce that they could be a character from a cartoon, a movie star, someone from history or a famous person.

c. The students mingle around asking other students questions about their identity, for example, 'Am I Australian?', 'Am I a female?', 'Am I in comedy movies?', 'Am I human?'. Students can only answer 'yes' or 'no' to these questions. If the other student answers 'yes', the questioner can ask another question of that student. If the answer is 'no', the student has to move on to another person in the group. The first student in the group to identify him or herself is the winner. The game may continue until all students have guessed their identities.

d. Reinforce listening, paying attention and remembering details. Discuss the outcome of the game with the students in the social circle.

Teacher preparation: *Collect magazines and newspapers for next lesson.*

Mastercopy 1: Listen ... who am I?

- Prince Charles
- Cathy Freeman
- Snoopy
- Jesus
- Harry Potter
- Spiderman
- Darth Vader
- Goldilocks
- Madonna
- Superman
- Kylie Minogue
- An alien from Mars
- Donald Duck
- Jerry Seinfeld
- Crocodile Dundee
- Bart Simpson
- Homer Simpson

Lesson 2: Similarities and differences

> **Outcomes**
> Students learn to:
> - be more aware of how others see them
> - appreciate people's similarities and differences
>
> **Resources**
> Magazines, newspapers
> Cardboard, glue
> Textas, pencils, scissors

Step 1

Social circle

a. Recap rules for social skills lessons and reinforce those who are following them. How can we help those who are having difficulty?
b. Review rules for meeting and getting to know people from the previous lesson. Stress the importance of paying attention and listening.
c. This lesson, we will be finding out more about each other, our similarities and differences, and how other people see us. What are ways in which people are different? Include likes and dislikes, race, language and abilities in discussion. These differences make us special, interesting and individual.

Step 2

Activity: Similarities and differences

a. Students in pairs cut out pictures from newspapers and magazines to identify particular characteristics about themselves: for example, their favourite sports team, food, colours, clothing, cars, animals, television characters, pop stars. They also ask their partners questions about their likes, and help each other find suitable pictures.
b. On cardboard, students design a collage about themselves, their likes and dislikes. Partners can help each other in their designs.
c. Students are invited to share their collages in the social circle, and describe themselves in relation to the pictures they chose. Discuss the many contrasts and likenesses between students.
d. These collages may be displayed around the room as a group collage entitled 'The class of 200–'. This is a group building activity.

Step 3

Game: Same ... different

a. A student stands in the middle of a circle of students seated on chairs. He or she identifies something they have in common with one or more students in the circle by observing them closely or looking at their collages, for instance, eye colour, shirt, pop group, pet, love of lasagne, favourite car.
b. Those students with that characteristic have to leave their seats and quickly find another seat in the circle, including the student in the centre. The student left without a seat takes the centre position and identifies a further characteristic in common with others. And so the game continues.
c. Discuss how exciting it is that we have differences as well as similarities, because our classroom and our lives could be quite boring otherwise!

Step 4

Extension activity: When we make mistakes

a. Sometimes we make quick judgments about people based on limited information, like seeing them in the street, in the newspaper or on TV, or hearing them on the radio, without really meeting and knowing them ourselves. This happens especially if they are obviously different from us, for example in race, language, age, appearance or abilities.
b. Teacher cuts out a picture from a magazine or newspaper of someone obviously different from the majority of class members. The picture is passed around for students to examine.
c. Ask students to write a paragraph about the person.
   - What sort of person do you think they are?
   - What might they do in life?
   - Would they be honest, serious, wealthy, kind, happy, healthy?
   - Would they make a good friend?
d. As a group, compare descriptions of the same person written by different students. They all can't be right! Discuss how we can make mistakes by judging people on the basis of limited information, especially race, clothes, appearance, perceived abilities or disabilities. This is a form of prejudice.
e. It seems that we need to pay more attention to people and to get to know more about them before we make decisions and judgments about them.

Teacher preparation: *Keep magazines for next lesson.*

Lesson 3: All eyes and ears

Outcomes
Students learn to:
> listen, look, remember and learn about others
> appreciate how mistakes are made by not listening
> follow rules for conversations

Resources
Magazine pictures, drawings
Paper, pencils
Messages on paper

Step 1

Social circle

a. We have learned a great deal about each other in the last two lessons, by paying attention to each other, including our similarities and differences.
b. This lesson we again use our eyes and ears to pay attention to what is happening around us, so we don't make mistakes, like we discussed in the previous lesson.

Step 2

Game: All eyes and ears!

a. Students form pairs. Student 1 chooses a picture from a magazine or his or her own drawings without student 2 seeing it. They sit down back to back. Student 1 describes the picture to student 2, who then draws the picture, listening carefully to the clues from student 1. Allow about 5 minutes for the description and the drawing. Students swap roles.
b. Both students show their drawings to each other and compare the drawings to the original pictures described.
c. As a group, discuss whether students made mistakes by not listening carefully to the description of the picture, or by not looking carefully enough at the picture in the first place.
d. Discuss with students. Has this ever happened to you?
   - Something you said was misheard by others and they got it wrong
   - Other people say that *you* don't listen and you get it wrong
   - You are talking about something you saw to someone who saw it too, but they describe it quite differently.

Alternative game: Get it right!

a. A student is given a message to read, such as, 'Sari was so upset when she heard that Adam's dog was knocked down by a truck on Saturday.' The students then pass the message around the circle by whispering it to each other. The last student in the circle recounts the message as they heard it. Then each student recounts what he or she had heard as the message was being passed around.

b. Discuss how much the message changes from one person to the next. Why does this happen?

c. Has this ever happened to you, that something you said was misheard by others? Or do other people say that you don't listen and you make mistakes that way? Fortunately, we are having plenty of practice at paying attention and listening carefully to make sure we all get it right!

Step 3

Discussion: Rules for conversations

a. How do we get the attention of someone we know to start a conversation?
- Choose a good time when they are not busy
- Approach them, smile
- Greet them and say their name
- Gain eye contact
- Be ready to say or ask something interesting.

b. How can we keep a conversation going with someone?
- Show them that you are listening by
  - staying still
  - maintaining eye contact
  - saying 'mm' or 'yes'
  - answering their questions
- Ask questions about them rather than just talking about yourself
- If they seem to get distracted, ask them if they are listening
- Finish the conversation nicely.

c. Students form pairs to practise these skills.

Unit 2: Look and listen for feelings

Aims

- To learn to use eyes and ears to find out about people's feelings
- To be aware of facial expression, voice tone and body gesture as cues to people's feelings
- To understand reasons for feelings and, therefore, behaviour
- To further develop a positive classroom culture which motivates children to learn pro-social skills and practise them in real life.

Lesson 4: Liking me, liking you

Outcomes
Students learn to:
- identify positive things about each other
- receive compliments
- set goals to improve social skills

Resources
Note paper
Pencils
4 empty tissue boxes
Worksheet 1

Step 1

Social circle

a. Discuss the concept of using our eyes and ears to find out what is happening around us and also information about other people. This lesson focuses on telling each other about the positive things we have learned about them.

b. Discuss compliments or positive comments. Request some examples of compliments students have been given by others or have given to others.

Step 2

Activity: Identifying 'good bits'

a. Suggest that everyone has something special about them, some 'good bits', something we could compliment them on. It might be their skills at sport or art, their great haircut, how they let you play tennis with them, how they say 'Hello', how they help you with maths, how they share their lunch, how good they are as class monitors. Sometimes we neglect to tell others the things we like about them. Often we just say the things we DON'T like about them. Let's find some 'good bits' about each other.

b. Ask for four volunteers from the class to have their names written on the tissue boxes to have compliments sent to them. Instruct all students (and teacher) to write a positive message to the nominated students. Allow them time to consider their comments before writing. Notes are placed in the boxes when finished.

c. Teacher may first check the notes in the boxes, and remove any negative ones without comment. The identified students can now read their compliments and, if they wish, share some with the group. This activity may be repeated until all students have had a compliments box filled by their classmates.

d. Discuss some of the compliments that are similar and some that are specific to particular students. Also discuss
   - What was it like to give positive comments to each other?
   - How do we give compliments to others?
     Smile, look at the person and speak sincerely.
   - What do you say when someone gives you a compliment?
     Smile, look at the person and say 'Thank you'.

Step 3

Exercise: What can I improve?

Students set goals for themselves, things that they would like to improve. Examples might include 'keep out of trouble', be better at maths', 'control my temper', 'make more friends', 'concentrate better'. Students record personal goals on Worksheet 1, to be reviewed in later lessons.

Step 4

Continuing activity: Reinforcing 'good bits' and improvements

a. Teachers should regularly encourage students to look for and comment on improvements they notice other students make.
b. This may be done formally via the compliments boxes. Students and teacher regularly record and post messages to classmates about positive things they have noticed. The names on the boxes are rotated through the roll, including the teacher's name.
c. Teachers may need to engineer helpful things for less popular children to do (such as running an errand, helping another student with a project), and then make a positive comment about it to the class and to the child through the post.
d. These messages may be saved to build a symbol of the new positive group culture, for example as bricks in a wall, leaves on a tree or links in a chain displayed in the room.
e. These 'good bits' exercises may be incorporated into formal social skills lessons or conducted at other times during the day, for example, in class meetings 15 minutes after lunch each day.

Worksheet 1: My goals

Setting my goals: Date ....

What would I like to improve in my behaviour, my work or my friends?

1. ....

2. ....

First review time: Date ....

How am I going with my goals?
Have I or anyone else noticed any improvements?

1. ....

2. ....

Second review time: Date ....

How am I going with my goals?
Have I or anyone else noticed any improvements?

1. ....

2. ....

More goals:

What else would I like to improve now?

1. ....

2. ....

I know I can improve anything if I work at it!

Lesson 5: Identifying feelings

Outcomes
Students learn to:
- develop skills of looking and listening for feelings
- identify face, body and voice cues for feelings
- identify a broad range of feelings

Resources
Worksheets 2 and 3

Step 1

Social circle

a. Review the previous lesson about compliments and setting goals to improve. Comment on positive things you have noticed some children doing or saying already. Ask 'How does it feel to hear nice things said about you? Do you feel proud people are noticing your good qualities? Do you feel liked, part of the group, safe and comfortable, happy to be at this school, or maybe a bit embarrassed?'
b. This lesson we will be talking about many feelings like these, and how to use our eyes and ears to identify them. On the board, brainstorm many feelings we can experience eg, scared, happy, sad, frustrated, bored, sleepy, angry, embarrassed.

Step 2

Activity: How can you tell?

a. Students form pairs. Hand out Worksheet 2 with faces showing a variety of feelings. Students examine the faces and identify the cues that tell us how each face is feeling. These cues will involve
- eyes
- mouth
- eyebrows
- brow.

Students demonstrate the face that goes with each feeling on the sheet.

b. To identify feelings, we also look at the bodily gestures including
- posture
- stance
- proximity to others
- hand gestures.

In pairs, students adopt the body position and posture which they think matches each feeling face on the worksheet.

c. We can also identify feelings by listening to people's tone of voice and words. For instance, if they speak louder and in a heavy voice they sound as if they are feeling angry, or if they speak faster and in a high voice they are possibly excited, or if they speak slowly and in a low tone they could sound sad. Demonstrate these examples in terms of pitch and volume of speech to convey different feelings.

d. Ask students to say the following statements to convey the alternative feelings listed, using different tones of voice, volume and pitch

    'Sorry'
        a. Sympathetic tone   b. Sarcastic tone

    'At last we won at football'
        a. Excited tone   b. Exasperated tone

    'No one cares about me'
        a. Sad tone   b. Angry tone

    'What shall I do now?'
        a. Worried tone   b. Offering to help tone

    'This is a great way to spend a weekend'
        a. Pleased tone   b. Sarcastic tone

    'I should have been more careful'
        a. Annoyed tone   b. Sad tone

e. Students think of other statements that may convey different feelings depending on how they are said.

f. If people are not sure about the feeling behind a spoken message, they generally use non-verbal cues (face and body gesture) to get it right.

Step 3

Exercise: Look and listen for feelings

Students complete Worksheet 3.

Teacher preparation: *Collect magazines and newspapers for next lesson.*

What is the program? 139

Worksheet 2: Feeling faces

Worksheet 3: Look and listen for feelings

Write a sentence that conveys the following feelings. Briefly sketch your face and body posture.

A sad feeling

....

....

A happy feeling

....

....

An angry feeling

....

....

A scared feeling

....

....

A worried feeling

....

....

An embarrassed feeling

....

....

Lesson 6: Reasons for feelings

Outcomes
Students learn to:
- understand the reasons for feelings
- appreciate that feelings vary between and within people

Resources
Newspapers, magazines
Worksheet 4
Box, stories on paper

Step 1

Social circle

a. As a class, review Worksheet 3. Check that students matched feelings with the appropriate facial expressions, body gestures and words.
b. This lesson deals with reasons for people's feelings (Why they feel like that), how feelings vary from person to person even in the same situations and how one person can have a mixture of feelings at the same time.

Step 2

Activity: Why do they feel like that?

a. In small groups, students find pictures in magazines showing people with various feelings in various situations. They discuss what might have happened to make them feel that way, that is, the reasons for their feelings.
b. As a class, discuss how people can have a mixture of feelings at one time. Students give examples of situations when they felt
- Sad and angry
  When you missed out on a treat, but your brother got one.
- Excited and scared
  You are on a fast ride at the fair.
- Proud and embarrassed
  You are accepting an award in front of the school.
- Pleased and worried
  You passed your music exam but think your friend may not.
- Excited, scared and disappointed
  You're waiting to see your favourite pop star; you're getting squashed in the crowd; you can't see over the crowd.

c. In addition, different people in the same situation can have quite different feelings. In small groups, students find and discuss examples in the pictures where different people in the same picture have different feelings.

Step 3

Exercise: Why I felt...?

Students complete Worksheet 4.

Step 4

Activity: Reasons for feelings charades

a. Teacher photocopies the list below and cuts it up into separate one-line stories (or writes them on cards) and places them in a box. For example
    - Your best friend is playing with a group and ignores you when you ask if you can join them
    - You have just watched a scary movie and you have to go bed alone; your sister laughs at you
    - Your teacher hands back your English test and your mark is very low; the student next to you has received the top mark
    - You are helping your dad set the table when you smash one of the family's best dinner plates
    - You have finally finished your homework and done well, then your little brother spills orange juice all over it
    - You are walking around the house complaining that there is nothing to do; your neighbour suggests that you smash bottles in the shed
    - You are looking everywhere for your pet dog, which is lost; your sister helps you look for it and she finds it.

b. Students in pairs pick a story from the box and devise a play around the storyline, out of sight of the class. They act out the play to the class in mime, using no speech. Their classmates watch carefully and guess what is happening, how they are feeling and why they might feel that way.

c. Discuss how different people in the story will have different feelings about the events, and that the main person may also have a mixture of feelings.

Teacher preparation: *Collect magazines for next lesson.*

Worksheet 4: Why I felt...?

Choose a feeling and write a story about what happened to make you feel like that.

I felt ....

because this happened

....
....
....
....
....

Did you have a mixture of feelings in that situation?

What feelings?

....

Did anyone else in the situation have different feelings from you?

Who?

....

What feelings did they seem to have?

....

How could you tell?

....

Unit 3: Communicating feelings

Aims

- To explore ways of being positive and making people feel better
- To understand the causal connection between feelings and behaviour
- To understand the bad habits people use to express their negative feelings to others
- To learn how to STOP the bad habits, control negative feelings and communicate positively
- To use the red traffic light cue and other reminders to STOP.

Lesson 7: Being positive

Outcomes
Students learn to:
> do and say positive things to others
> help others feel better

Resources
Magazines
Cardboard, glue, scissors
Worksheet 5

Step 1

Social circle

a. Review the skills learned in previous lessons about feelings
   - Understand that different people have different feelings … and that's okay
   - Understand your own feelings and the reasons you feel that way
   - Keep your eyes and ears open to pick up feeling cues from others
   - If you're not sure, don't guess; ask them more questions to get it right.
b. In this lesson we learn more about making other people feel better by doing and saying positive things.

Step 2

Exercise: Making people feel better

a. When someone is worried or upset or angry about something, even if it doesn't involve us and we cannot solve the problem for them, we can help them feel better. Students brainstorm ways, for example

   - Approach them, talk to them
   - Listen to them
   - Acknowledge their feelings (*'Yeah, I wouldn't like that either'*)
   - Do or say something positive
   - Offer to help if you can.

b. We can also make others feel better by responding positively to their requests if they are reasonable. For example, adults often ask children to help them by following instructions or doing jobs. You can respond positively by

   - Saying 'Yes, okay'
   - If you're not sure what is being requested of you, ask the adult to please explain

- Do it quickly and properly so you don't have to do it again
- If you have a good reason for not doing it, discuss it with the adult.

c. Students work in pairs to complete Worksheet 5. Discuss as a class.

Step 3

Activity: Being positive in class

a. We all enjoy some activities on our own. It's okay that we do not need to be with other people all of the time. But sometimes, we feel lonely and left out without people to do things with. Students brainstorm what they like to do by themselves and what they like to do with other people.

b. Do some students in our class feel lonely and left out at times? Here is a task to do together and practise including everyone. Organise the class into groups of six students. Each group selects a large picture from a magazine, pastes it on to cardboard, and cuts out a jigsaw of six interesting shapes. The jigsaw pieces are then passed on to another group for novelty. Each student in a group takes one jigsaw piece and takes turns trying to fit their piece to complete the jigsaw.

c. In the social circle, discuss
- How did you feel waiting for your turn?
- How would you have felt if your piece didn't fit?
- Did anyone help you with your piece?
- If they did, how did that make you feel?
- Did anyone in your group feel left out?

d. Brainstorm ways to include all students in the classroom and the play area. Write the ideas on the display board. Encourage students to add to the list at any time.

e. Making people feel better in our class is about paying attention, reading how people feel, listening to them and involving them.

Worksheet 5: Making people feel better

What can you do or say to make these people feel better?

Your sister is crying because she is afraid to go to the dentist.

I could

....

Your classmate is in the school play and he forgets his lines.

I could

....

Your father has just lost his job.

I could

....

Your friend is scared to go home because her father hits her for being late.

I could

....

A new child at school is being bullied by others.

I could

....

Your teacher is annoyed because the students are not paying attention.

I could

....

Your mother is very upset because grandma is sick.

I could

....

Your friend is crying because he can't get to sleep at the school camp.

I could

....

Lesson 8: STOP the bad habits

Outcomes
Students learn to:
- understand feelings as the cause of behaviour
- identify negative feelings in problem situations
- identify bad habits they use with others
- understand the STOP steps

Resources
STOP – Traffic light poster
Mastercopy 2, pencils, Textas
STOP and THINK Friendship video/workbook (optional)

Step 1

Social circle
Last lesson focused on being positive. This lesson focuses on the way we show our negative feelings to others. When we are upset or angry, these negative feelings cause us to behave in negative ways or 'bad habits'.

Step 2

Story/role-play: Bad habits

a. Instruct students to close their eyes and imagine the following story. For more impact, students role-play the story convincingly.

Carly was popular at her old school. But she felt lonely at her new one. One day, some children asked her to meet them at the canteen. When she arrived, they weren't there. She saw them on the oval. They laughed as she approached them. She yelled abuse at them.

b. Discuss issues
- How was Carly feeling? Why was she feeling like that? How could you tell?
- How were the other children feeling? Why? How could you tell?
- How did Carly show her feelings? What bad habits did she use?
- Did it make the problem better or worse?
- Do you use bad habits like Carly when people upset you?

Alternative resource: *Friendship* video: Bad habits

Teacher instructions: *Scenes in the video are identified by a number and a page in the 'Shooting Script' of the workbook accompanying the video.*

a. Show students Scene 1 from the video, p. 39 in the script, where Brent is ignored when he asks to play basketball. Stop tape at the end of Scene 1.
b. Discuss this scene
   - How was Brent feeling? Why was he feeling like that? How could you tell?
   - How were the other children feeling? Why? How could you tell?
   - How did he show his feelings? What bad habits did he use?
   - Did it make the problem better or worse?
   - Do you use bad habits like Brent when children don't let you play?

Step 3

Discussion: The STOP steps

a. Fortunately, everyone can change bad habits. They just have to STOP first when they are upset or angry, like cars stop at the red traffic light to avoid accidents. Discuss traffic lights on the roads
   - Why do we have them?
   - What do the different colours mean?
   - Why don't cars just keep on going when the light shines red?

b. You can apply the same rules to problems you have with other people. Point to the STOP poster. The red light reminds you of the first step to take when you have a problem with someone

   - STOP the bad habits. Don't let your feelings take over. Wait.
   - Look and listen instead. Use your eyes and ears to work out

   What is the problem… What is actually happening?
   What are the feelings… How are all the people involved feeling?
   These are the questions you ask yourself at the STOP step.

c. If the *Friendship* video is available, play the video from Scene 2, p.40, to the end of Scene 4, p.46, where Brent is about to join in the game without using bad habits this time. Point to the STOP poster. Discuss the STOP step Bonez taught Brent using the words in point b. above.

d. Previous social skills lessons have taught us how to look and listen to find out information. Now we can use these skills to solve problems with other people.

Step 4

Activity: Personal traffic light poster: STOP

Hand out copies of Mastercopy 2. Students design their own STOP poster (or generate one on the computer) to store in their folder or reduce in size to make a badge or card which may be laminated and worn/carried as a reminder to STOP.

Mastercopy 2: STOP poster

Lesson 9: Reminders to STOP

Outcomes
Students learn to:
- recognise their bad habits
- practise the STOP steps
- understand and use reminders

Resources
STOP poster
Scissors, pencils, paper
Coloured string, paint
Worksheet 6
Worksheet 1 (first review)
Parent Information 1
STOP and THINK Friendship video (optional)

Step 1

Exercise: My bad habits

Remind students how Carly or Brent in the previous lesson did not solve their problem by using bad habits like yelling and abusing. We all use bad habits at times. Hand out Worksheet 6 for students to complete.

Step 2

Story/role-play: STOP first

a. In the social circle, ask for volunteers to discuss bad habits they use when they are feeling angry or upset.
b. Fortunately, we can change our bad habits by following the STOP steps. Remind students of Carly's story in the previous lesson. Introduce this element

   As Carly was approaching the group on the oval, Joe cracked a joke. The other children were not actually laughing at her.

c. Students form small groups and design role-plays where Carly doesn't use bad habits. She stops first, controls her feelings, looks and listens to find out what is *really* happening and how people are feeling, as we learned to do.
d. In the social circle, discuss
   - Did stopping first work better for Carly?
   - Do you think it is strong or weak for Carly to control her feelings?
   - How likely is she to forget next time she is upset or angry?

Alternative resource: *Friendship* video: STOP first

a. Show the video from Scene 5, p. 47, where Brent tries again to join in. Stop the tape at the end of Scene 8, p. 48, after Bonez discusses reminders.
b. Students may role-play this scene to practise the STOP steps. Discuss
   - What worked for Brent? (Controlling his feelings, looking and listening to find out what was happening and about people's feelings – like we have learned to do)
   - Do you think it is strong or weak for Brent to control his feelings?
   - How likely is he to forget next time he is upset or angry?
   - Has this happened to you? Have you tried hard to control yourself in a situation and it worked, but you blew it the next time?

Step 3

Activity: Reminders to STOP

a. Reminders help us remember things. The red light is a reminder to STOP, control our feelings, look and listen to work out what is happening, just like the red light reminds drivers. Students have their own personal STOP poster from last lesson to stick on their desk or reduce to wear or carry.
b. There are many other reminders they can use, things that attract their attention so they notice them. Students brainstorm ideas for reminders, such as wearing a friendship band, a special key-ring or toy in your pocket, putting coloured tape on pencils, painting a fingernail, saying a special word to yourself, counting slowly, taking three deep breaths or having the STOP symbol around your play area secretly. Teachers can also be 'reminders' to students by quietly saying something like 'Remember the red light' if children are using bad habits.
c. In small groups, students design and make reminders, for example friendship bracelets by plaiting coloured string, sticking coloured tape or paper around their pencils or making a 'secret' STOP signal with their Mastercopy 2 poster. When the reminder's novelty (and hence, its effectiveness) wears off, students choose another reminder until they feel in control themselves.

Step 4

Exercise: Am I improving?

Students refer back to Worksheet 1 for a formal review of their progress towards achieving their goals, as identified in Lesson 4. Students will have received feedback from teacher and classmates about their 'good bits' and this is recorded on their goal sheets plus their opinions. This is an individual or small group exercise.

Parent information

Students take Parent Information 1 home with their Social Skills folder to discuss with their parents. Remind students to return their folders the following day.

Worksheet 6: STOP the bad habits!

Describe a time when your feelings took over and you used bad habits ... and the problem got worse!

This was the problem at the start

....

....

....

How did you feel?

....

What did you want to happen?

....

....

Then your feelings took over and what happened next?

....

....

....

Could it have worked out better if you had STOPPED first and not let your feelings take over?

....

Parent Information 1: What your child is learning

In STOP THINK DO social skills lessons, the children are currently learning

- To get to know themselves and their classmates better
- To notice positive things and compliment each other
- To pay attention, listen and talk to each other
- To identify and communicate their feelings appropriately
- To control their negative feelings and STOP using bad habits
- To remember the red traffic light and other reminders as cues to STOP.

What can you do to help your child learn these valuable skills?

- When children are learning new skills, it is very helpful for their parents to talk with them about what they are learning
- Parents can also look for and praise any positive changes in their child's behaviour and attitudes
- You may check your child's Social Skills folder and discuss the exercises with them; this folder needs to be returned to school *tomorrow*
- If you would like to discuss this program with your child's teacher, please make an appointment.

Unit 4: Solving social problems

Aims

- To build on the STOP steps where eyes and ears are used to identify problems and feelings. At THINK, the brain is the key!
- To learn cognitive problem solving skills (brainstorming and consequential thinking) at THINK, signalled by the yellow traffic light
- To understand that social problems are solved by STOPPING and THINKING about options and possible consequences *before* acting
- To learn shorthand terms like Cool, Weak and Aggro, which will help evaluate options and consequences.

Lesson 10: Use your brain

> **Outcomes**
> Students learn to:
> - experiment with reminders to STOP
> - appreciate that their brain loves to THINK
> - brainstorm options to solve social problems
> - put thinking between feeling and acting
>
> **Resources**
> STOP and THINK posters
> Mastercopy 3, pencils, Textas
> Large sheet of paper *or* display board
> *STOP and THINK Friendship* video (optional)

Step 1

Social circle

a. Discuss reminders students have found useful to help them control their feelings and behaviour, and what they did instead of bad habits.

b. This lesson focuses on what to do after we STOP and control our feelings. Point to the THINK poster. We are at the yellow light, which reminds drivers to get their car into gear ready to go, but not go yet. At THINK, we use our **brains** to think about options and consequences – all the things we could try to solve problems, before we actually do anything. There are millions of ways to solve problems. The more we use our brains to THINK, the smarter we get. Brains love to think!

Step 2

Story/role-play: Using their brains

a. Ask students to imagine this scenario and role-play for impact

   Ali is tired after a late night. At sports day the next day, he doesn't want to let his team down in the relay race. Everyone is urging him on. But he drops the baton as he passes it to Carol. She puts him down. Ali slumps to the ground in tears and blames Carol.

b. Discuss the STOP steps: What is happening? How are the people feeling?

c. Now to THINK. Point to poster. *What could they try?* Ask children to brainstorm the various options Ali (and Carol) could try to solve the problem. Record options for display, such as
   - He could cry like he did. Or he could blame Carol like he did
   - Or he could push her over

- Or he could say 'Sorry'; he will try to do better in the next race
- Or he could walk calmly away and forget it. Or …

The aim is to come up with as many options as possible; don't discourage any ideas, no matter how 'silly'. Reinforce students for their 'Good thinking', 'Your brains are hot!' Some suggestions may be role-played.

Alternative resource: *Friendship* video: Using their brains

a. Show the video from the beginning of Scene 9, p. 49, to the middle of Scene 11, p. 52, where Bonez blocks his ears as Sophie sings. He calls 'Enough!'.
b. Recap STOP steps: What is happening? How are people feeling?
c. Now to THINK. Point to poster. *What could they try?* On a display board or large sheet of paper, list the various options Sophie thinks of to solve the problem with Max. Students brainstorm more suggestions (also for Max). The aim is to come up with as many ideas as possible; don't discourage any, no matter how 'silly'. Reinforce students: 'Good thinking', 'Your brains are hot!' Role-play some suggestions.

Step 3

Discussion: Types of options

a. Suggest that the options students brainstormed on the board probably fall into the following categories or types. Record on board as well
   - Stand up for self nicely: ask or speak nicely, compromise, share
   - Ignore: walk away, do something else
   - Get upset: cry, sulk
   - Whinge to an adult
   - Use physical force: hit, grab, push, kick
   - Use verbal abuse: yell, swear, threaten, blame.
b. The class is divided into small groups. They study the display of options for Ali or Sophie. Each group finds examples to fit each category above. One member of each group records for the group.
c. In the social circle, teacher calls out categories. The recorders give examples of options found by their group to fit the categories. If a category has no examples, students think of some to fit.

Step 4

Activity: Personal traffic light poster: THINK

Hand out copies of Mastercopy 3. Students design their own THINK poster (or generate one on the computer) to store in their folder or reduce in size to make a badge or card which may be laminated and worn/carried, as a reminder to use their brain and THINK of answers before they do anything.

Teacher instruction: *Retain list of options for Lessons 11, 12 and 16.*

Mastercopy 3: THINK poster

THINK

Lesson 11: Cool, Weak, Aggro

Outcomes
Students learn to:
> THINK about options in terms of Cool, Weak and Aggro categories
> differentiate Cool, Weak and Aggro options

Resources
THINK poster
Worksheets 7 and 8
List of options (from previous lesson)

Step 1

Social circle

a. Refer students to the first step on the THINK poster, the long list of options they thought up to solve Ali's or Sophie's problem in the previous lesson, and the examples of categories or types of options they identified.
b. In this lesson, we describe these categories in shorthand terms like Cool, Weak and Aggro, to help us remember them and think of them quickly (point to THINK poster).
c. Children usually understand Aggro ways, so it is a good place to start.
   - Options involving verbal or physical force are examples of the **Aggro** way. Demonstrate a 'clenched fist'.
   - Options involving upset emotions or whingeing to adults are examples of the **Weak** way. Demonstrate a 'thumbs down' sign.
   - Options involving positive attitudes and behaviours, standing up nicely for yourself or ignoring are examples of the **Cool** way. Demonstrate a 'thumbs up' sign.

Step 2

Role-play: Cool, Weak, Aggro

a. Call out some options from the brainstorm list. Students demonstrate the hand signal to match the option as it is identified. They will not always agree on signs. The characteristics of Cool, Weak and Aggro need to be described more precisely, as in Worksheet 7.
b. Ask students to select an Aggro way from the list of options (such as kicking out at the person). Some students role-play this option. Ask the other students to describe how the character looks, sounds and feels. Check Worksheet 7 for further descriptions of the Aggro way.

c. Students then select a Weak option (for example, whingeing to an adult) from the brainstorm list and role-play it. Other students describe how the character looks, sounds and feels. Check Worksheet 7 for further characteristics of the Weak way.
d. Students then select a Cool option (for instance, ignoring the person and joining with friends) and role-play it. Others describe how the character looks, sounds and feels. Check Worksheet 7 for characteristics of the Cool way.
e. However, there is no absolute differentiation of these categories. For example, a young child may say that it is Cool to tell an adult if they have a problem, while an older child may think that it is Weak or even Aggro; it all depends on how they feel, look and act when they tell the adult. The main point is for students to be thinking about such categories as short-cut ways to finding options, rather than being too precise about the categories.
f. Regarding telling an adult about teasing, stress that children who are being seriously bullied, harassed or frightened need to speak to an adult because they cannot solve this problem themselves; this is not Weak.

Step 3

Exercise: Cool, Weak, Aggro ways

Students work in pairs or small groups to discuss examples on Worksheet 8 and complete it. Groups may role play their answers for more impact.

Teacher instruction: *Retain list of options for next lesson.*

Worksheet 7: Descriptions of Cool, Weak and Aggro

How we look, sound and feel when we behave in the following ways

Cool	Weak	Aggro
stay calm	sulk	abuse
in control	give in	out of control
stand straight	slump over	stand close
eye contact	look down	glare
speak firmly but friendly	mumble	yell
confident	unconfident	threaten
feel okay	feel upset	feel angry
compromise	cry	kick
bargain	whinge	blame
share	sigh	hit
ask nicely	dob	tease
politely assertive	passive	aggressive
ignore		

Worksheet 8: Cool, Weak, Aggro ways

Your teacher doesn't choose you to be class monitor this week.
What is an Aggro way of behaving?

....

What is a Weak way?

....

What is a Cool way?

....

Your friend chooses to play with another group at lunchtime.
What is an Aggro way of reacting?

....

What is a Weak way?

....

What is a Cool way?

....

Someone blames you for something you didn't do.
What is an Aggro way of reacting?

....

What is a Weak way?

....

What is a Cool way?

....

You're watching your best TV program and your brother changes the channel.
What is an Aggro way of behaving?

....

What is a Weak way?

....

What is a Cool way?

....

Lesson 12: THINK about consequences

Outcomes

Students learn to:
- consider possible consequences of options
- understand that Cool ways often have better consequences

Resources

THINK poster
Worksheet 9
List of options (from previous lesson)
Social problems in Appendix (p. 207) displayed or photocopied
STOP and THINK Friendship video (optional)

Step 1

Social circle

a. Review Cool, Weak or Aggro options for trying to solve problems. Check that students understand these concepts and the characteristics of each.
b. But how do we know which option is the best one? This lesson focuses on using our brain to THINK about the likely consequences of each option. Point to the THINK poster. *What might happen then?* Thinking about consequences will help us decide which to choose.

Step 2

Story/role-play: Consequences!!!

a. Remind students of the story of Ali and the list of Cool, Weak and Aggro options students thought of for resolving the problem with Carol.
b. Select an Aggro option from the list (such as screaming at Carol). Ask students
   'What might happen if he tried that option?'
c. Brainstorm possible consequences and record them on the board or paper to retain. These may be role-played in small groups. Ask students how they feel about these consequences
   'Would you be happy with that outcome?'
d. Similarly, select a Weak option (for example, sulking) and then a Cool option (for example, standing up for oneself positively) from the list. Ask questions as above.
e. Students brainstorm possible consequences, which are recorded and some are role-played. Check how students feel about these consequences.
f. Compare the likely consequences of the Cool, Weak and Aggro ways.

- Aggro ways generally make people aggro back

- Weak ways make people ignore or laugh at them
- Cool ways often get friendly reactions and positive consequences.

Alternative resource: *Friendship* video: Consequences!!!

a. Show the video from the middle of Scene 11, p. 52, from Bonez's comment 'Let's go through some of your options and check out the consequences' to the end of p. 53, after Sophie wins the garden gnome.

b. Select one of Sophie's Aggro options from the list (for instance, screaming at Max). Ask students

   'What might happen if she tried that option?'

   Brainstorm possible consequences and write them on the board or paper to retain. These may be role-played in small groups. Ask students how they feel about these consequences

   'Would you be happy with that outcome?'

c. Similarly, select a Weak option (for instance, crying) and then a Cool option (for instance, making a deal with Max that he can have his turn after her) from the list. Ask students to brainstorm possible consequences, record them and role-play some. Check how students feel about these consequences.

d. Compare the likely consequences of the Cool, Weak and Aggro ways.

- Aggro ways generally make people aggro back
- Weak ways make people ignore or laugh at them
- Cool ways often get friendly reactions and positive consequences.

Step 3

Exercise: Options and consequences

a. Hand out Worksheet 9. The list of social problems in the Appendix (p. 207) is photocopied or displayed for students.

b. Students choose a conflict from the list. They work individually, in pairs or small groups to work out options and consequences for the chosen problem and complete the worksheet. Conflict situations, options and consequences may be role-played.

Teacher instruction: *Retain*

   a. *List of social problems from Appendix (p. 207) for next lesson*
   b. *Lists of options and consequences (Ali/Sophie) for Lesson 16.*

Worksheet 9: THINK about options and consequences

STOP

What is the problem? (Choose one from the list)

....

How are you feeling about it?

....

How is the other person feeling about it?

....

You have stopped to work out what is happening and how people are feeling. Now it's time to use your brain and

THINK

What options can you try to solve this problem?

1. You could ....

Is that Cool, Weak or Aggro? ....

OR
2. You could ....

Is that Cool, Weak or Aggro? ....

What might happen if you try these options?

What might happen if you tried the *first* idea?

a. ....

OR b. ....

What might happen if you tried the *second* idea?

a. ....

OR b. ....

Now think of a really, really Cool option.

What consequences might that option have?

a. ....

OR b. ....

Whoa! Your brain is really sizzling!

Unit 5: The cool and friendly way

Aims

- To appreciate that the Cool way generally leads to more acceptable consequences
- To learn the Friendly way – stepping into other people's shoes to see it from their perspective, being fair, considerate, respectful
- To understand that the Friendly way is usually compatible with the Cool way
- To consider many people's feelings and consequences in very tricky problems that involve a moral dilemma
- To learn the Co-operative way to behave when people belong to a group – Co-operative = Cool + Friendly.

Lesson 13: Thumbs up for Cool and Friendly

Outcomes
Students learn to:
- use Cool ways for more acceptable consequences
- consider other people – the Friendly way
- understand that Cool is often Friendly

Resources
STOP and THINK posters
List of social problems (from previous lesson)
Worksheet 10
STOP and THINK Friendship video (optional)

Step 1

Social circle

a. Review the likely consequences of using Cool, Weak or Aggro ways to solve social problems.

b. This lesson focuses on Cool ways to behave, since they are likely to have better consequences. We will also talk about Friendly ways – stepping into other people's shoes and considering their feelings. Point to poster. Cool and Friendly ways often go together.

Step 2

Discussion and role-play: Thumbs up for Cool

a. Ask students to picture the following

You are working on an electronics model for a school display. Your classmate is talking to someone else and without thinking, knocks the model on the floor, breaking it.

b. Pointing to the posters to guide the STOP and THINK steps, ask students
- What is happening in this story? How would you feel?
- What options could you try to solve the problem? Is each option Cool, Weak or Aggro?
- THINK of Cool ways where you stand up for yourself but you remain calm and in control
- This is also likely to be Friendly to the other person, because you are not getting angry or emotional at them and you are behaving respectfully to them. You treat them like you want to be treated.

c. Role-play Cool and Friendly options to this conflict in small groups. Other conflicts may be chosen and discussed or role-played, as above.
d. Brainstorm the rules for behaving in Cool and Friendly ways in conflicts, for example
    - Face the other person, give eye contact and stand straight
    - Stay calm and in control
    - Speak in a firm but friendly manner
    - If the person made a mistake, calmly explain what happened
    - Listen to the person's response
    - If you made a mistake, apologise
    - Discuss a solution; be prepared to compromise.

Additional resource: *Friendship* video: Cool and Friendly

a. Replay the short Scene 5, p. 47, where Brent acts Cool to join the game. Ask the students to comment on the verbal, non-verbal and emotional characteristics of Brent's Cool and Friendly way. Replay the clip a number of times to check.
b. Students discuss further Cool and Friendly options Brent or the other children in the story could try to resolve this issue. These may be role-played for practice in Cool and Friendly ways.

Step 3

Exercise: Cool it!

Students complete Worksheet 10, which presents examples of
- How to make requests the Cool way
- How to ask for help the Cool way
- How to accept a reasonable 'No' for an answer the Cool way
- How to make complaints the Cool way
- How to handle fair or unfair criticisms the Cool way.

Worksheet 10: Cool it!

You want to go to a scary movie but you don't think your parents will let you.

A Cool way to make a request is to

....

Your father criticises you for leaving your bike in the driveway because he nearly drove over it in the dark.

A Cool way to handle reasonable criticism is to

....

You lent your skateboard to your friend and he returns it with a big scratch on it.

A Cool way to make a complaint is to

....

Your friend asks to borrow $5 from you but she still owes you money.

A Cool way to say 'No' is to

....

Your teacher is really busy helping another student but you need his help.

A Cool way to ask for help is to

....

A shop assistant blames you for knocking over a biscuit display. But you didn't.

A Cool way to handle unfair criticism is to

....

Lesson 14: Very tricky moral problems

Outcomes
Students learn to:
- use be aware of the pressure friends can put on them
- use consider the feelings of people who may not be present
- use use their brains in moral dilemmas

Resources
STOP and THINK posters
Worksheet 11

Step 1

Social circle

a. Introduce the concept of very tricky problems when there is a moral issue about right and wrong. In these situations, we need to think about what is good for us (Cool) and what is good for our friend (Friendly).

b. But we also need to think about other people who are not even present at the time. What would our parents, teachers, other adults like police or an important friend feel or say or do if we chose a particular option? We need to consider these consequences as well. Wow, this will test our brains!

Step 2

Discussion: A very tricky moral problem

a. Ask students to close their eyes and imagine the following situation.

   Mia and Kelly have been friends for a long time. Lately, Kelly has been hanging around with a group of other girls. Mia would like to join the group as well. One day they are in a shop and Mia sees Kelly take a silver chain from a display and put it in her pocket. She tells Mia that people have to steal something to join the group.

b. Following the STOP and THINK posters, discuss this situation.
   - STOP and find out what actually happened
   - How does Mia feel?
   - How does Kelly feel?
   - THINK about what Mia could do? Is this Cool, Weak or Aggro?
   - What could Kelly do? Is this Cool, Weak or Aggro?
   - Is it a FRIENDLY thing to do, considering the other person?

c. BUT there are more people than just each other for Mia and Kelly to consider. They should think

- Is it a Friendly thing to do to the shop owner, whom they know?
- What about their parents, if they knew they had stolen?
- What about their teachers? How do they feel about thieves?
- What about their other friends?

Their brains will really be smoking with this tricky problem!

Extension discussion: Staying out of trouble

a. Emphasise to students that while it is difficult to consider everyone in these tricky problems, using your brains to STOP and THINK about options and consequences is likely to help you stay out of trouble.

b. Behaving in a Friendly way does not necessarily mean that your friend will like your choice of option, especially if you are saying 'No' to them. It does mean that you have considered your friend's position but you may have a different opinion about what is good for them. The same applies to all the people that you have considered when thinking about what to do.

c. Very tricky problems often involve weighing up short- and long-term consequences. What might seem easy or fun or tempting to do at the time might have serious negative results later, for instance, affect your health, get you in trouble with the law, get you suspended from school or cost a lot of money to fix.

d. Various moral dilemmas may be discussed, such as situations involving pressure to set fires, vandalise places, take or sell drugs, lie, cheat. Teachers discuss at a level to suit the students' age and maturity.

Step 3

Exercise: A very tricky problem to solve

Complete Worksheet 11. This may be done as an individual or group activity.

Teacher preparation: *Collect magazines and newspapers for next lesson.*

Worksheet 11: A very tricky problem

STOP

The problem: You are sleeping over at your friend Ben's house. His parents go out for a while. Ben pleads with you to drink some of his parents' alcohol with him. He says you are a wimp if you don't.

The feelings: You are a bit shocked and scared. Your friend is excited but getting frustrated.

THINK

What could you do?

1. ....

2. ....

3. ....

What might happen if you tried these options?

1. ....

2. ....

3. ....

But there are other people to consider too

What would Ben's parents feel and do if you stole their alcohol?
....

What would your mother feel and do if you took drugs like alcohol?
....

What about your swimming mates who think alcohol ruins your health? What would they say or do if they knew?
....

How can you stand up for yourself and say NO to your friend in a Cool way
AND still take care of your friend's feelings in a Friendly way
AND also consider his and your parents, and your swimming team?

....

Lesson 15: Co-operative = Cool + Friendly

Outcomes
Students learn to:
- understand that we all belong to groups
- value groups functioning well
- use co-operative ways in groups (i.e. Cool + Friendly ways)

Resources
Role cards with instructions
Parent Information 2

Step 1

Social circle

a. What do students understand by the word *co-operation*? List their ideas on the board.
b. This lesson looks at Cool and Friendly ways for co-operating in groups.

Step 2

Group activity: A team effort

a. Ask for seven volunteers from the class to take part in a team activity. They sit in a circle. Each randomly takes a card, reads it and then assumes the role described on the card. The roles include

- The Leader, who starts the discussion and keeps everyone on task
- The Clown, who mucks around and makes others laugh
- The Yes person, who agrees with everyone else
- The Loudmouth, who talks too much and interrupts others
- The Cop Out, who switches off and does not join in
- The Put Down, who embarrasses and criticises others
- The Bright Spark, who comes up with many exciting ideas.

b. The team is presented with a task, for example

This team has won a school award and $20 for their performance in a debating competition. Decide as a group how to spend the money.

Encourage students to act out their roles convincingly during this group discussion. Allow the discussion to continue for about 5 minutes, with other students observing closely.

c. Ask observers to comment on the various roles that the team members played and how helpful they were in terms of reaching a group decision. Discuss how this team is not likely to reach a decision because of the destructive roles some members played; they certainly were not being co-operative. Repeat the activity with new team members and tasks.

Alternative group activity: Co-operation *Rules!*

Students design a large poster for the class entitled 'Co-operation *Rules!*' where they list the most important rules for a successful group, for example

- Everyone has a chance to speak and give their ideas
- Say your ideas in a Cool way
- Others should listen: ask them politely to listen if they are distracted
- Treat others like you want to be treated – the Friendly way
- If there is disagreement, STOP and THINK to solve the problem by discussing options and consequences as a group
- If a group task is being planned, work out each person's role (who is doing what) and the timeline (when things need to be done).

Step 3

Discussion: Co-operative = Cool + Friendly

a. For groups to work well, the people in the group cannot always have their own way or there would be constant hassles and nothing would get done. They also have to consider other group members' feelings and views. This means a combination of Cool and Friendly behaviour. This is the Co-operative way in groups. If students had used these techniques in our team effort earlier, they may have succeeded in the task of working out what to do with the $20!

b. Usually groups have some rules to guide people to co-operate, like the rules we use for our social skills lessons. Brainstorm types of groups that students know about or belong to, such as sporting, social, family, school, musical or religious groups. Discuss what rules the groups have for ensuring the co-operation of members and how the groups would not work if the members did not co-operate.

Parent information

Distribute Parent Information 2 for students to take home with their Social Skills folder to discuss with their parents. Remind them to return folders to school the following day.

Parent Information 2: What your child is learning

In STOP THINK DO social skills lessons, the children are currently learning

- To think of many ways to solve problems with other people
  Some are Cool, some are Weak, some are Aggro ways
- To try Cool ways because they have better consequences
  Cool means standing up for yourself in a positive way
- Cool ways are usually Friendly
  Friendly means considering other people's feelings and views
- To use Co-operative ways in groups so that they function well
  Co-operative means Cool + Friendly
- To remember the yellow traffic light as a cue to THINK.

What can you do to help your child learn these valuable skills?

- When children are learning new skills, it is very helpful for their parents to talk with them about what they are learning
- Parents can also look for and praise any positive changes in their child's behaviour and attitudes
- You may check your child's Social Skills folder and discuss the exercises with your child; this folder needs to be returned to school *tomorrow*
- If you would like to discuss this program with your child's teacher, please make an appointment.

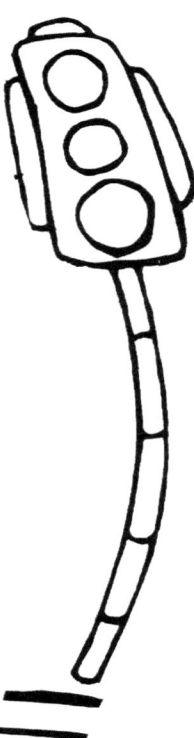

Unit 6: DOing it!

Aims

- To choose options that have the best likely consequences at DO, as signalled by the green traffic light
- To learn behavioural skills for putting chosen options into practice
- To fine-tune students' bodies so they send the right signals to others
- To practise skills for making and keeping friends.

Lesson 16: Fine-tune your body

Outcomes
Students learn to:
- choose options with the best consequences
- put chosen options into action using voice, facial and distance cues

Resources
STOP THINK DO posters
Mastercopy 4, pencils, Textas
List of options/consequences (from Lesson 12)
Worksheet 12
STOP and THINK Friendship video (optional)

Step 1

Social circle

On the posters, remind students that we use eyes and ears at STOP and brains at THINK. Now we are up to the DO steps. The green light is on. It tells the car driver to go and it tells us to DO something. We choose the option with the best consequences and put it into action, sending the right signals with the **body.**

Step 2

Story/role-play: Fine-tuning his body

a. Refer to the lists of options and consequences discussed for Ali in earlier lessons. Point to DO poster. *What is the best option?* After weighing up the consequences of various options, students choose the best one, that is, the one with the most acceptable consequences. A majority vote may be taken to decide which option to DO. This is likely to be a Cool option (such as, standing up positively for himself).

b. But to solve the problem effectively, Ali must do it properly so he sends the right signals to Carol. *How would he do it?* Point to poster. He has to fine-tune his body in terms of his
- facial expressions
- tone of voice and volume
- distance he stands from her.

c. Students role-play this option a number of times using the *same* words (for instance, 'Please don't speak to me like that; I *am* sorry') BUT varying the elements of voice, face and distance. In different role-plays, Ali alters
- the facial cues – sulks or glares or frowns
- the voice cues – whispers or yells or speaks very quickly
- the distance cues – stands too close or too far away.

After each variation, discuss how the actor playing Carol in the role-play feels and how she would respond if someone gave her this signal. Would it solve the original problem or could it make it worse?

Alternative resource: *Friendship* video: Fine-tuning her body

a. Show the video from the beginning of p. 54 in script (after Bonez congratulated Sophie on being a winner) to the end of Scene 12, p. 56.
b. After weighing up the consequences of various options, Sophie finally chose a Cool option of asking Max nicely to wait his turn. She must do this option properly so she sends the right signals to Max. And it worked!
c. BUT let's imagine that she gave Max the wrong signals with her voice or face or distance cues.
d. Students role-play Scene 12 a number of times, each time varying face, voice or distance while still using the *same* words as Sophie uses in the script. In different role-plays, Sophie alters
   - the distance cues – stands too close or too far away or sits down
   - the voice cues – whispers or yells or speaks very quickly
   - the facial cues – sulks or glares or frowns.

After each variation, discuss how the actor playing Max feels and how he would respond if someone gave him this signal. Could it make it worse?

Step 3

Exercise: Doing it well

a. Hand out Worksheet 12. Read out the problem. Students imagine the scenario and role-play it. If the STOP and THINK Friendship video is available, show Scene 14, p. 57, where this scenario is repeated twice to reinforce details.
b. Students form groups of three. One child has the role of Noni, another is Brent and the third is Wendy. Each member of the group gives their feelings and options in their role and records them on the worksheet. They discuss possible consequences of these options as a group.
c. At DO, each group chooses their best option. If they do not all agree, they find an acceptable compromise that they will all try, or they vote and go with the majority. In groups of three, they decide how to put their chosen option into action in terms of face, voice and distance cues next lesson.

Step 4

Activity: Personal traffic light poster: DO

Hand out copies of Mastercopy 4. Students design their DO poster (or generate one on the computer) to store in their folder or reduce in size to make a badge or card which may be laminated and worn/carried as a reminder to DO it well!

Worksheet 12: Doing it well

STOP

What is the problem?

Children are playing basketball. Noni misses the ball and is teased by others, especially Wendy. Brent tries to support her.

What are the feelings?

How does Noni feel? ....

How does Wendy feel? ....

How does Brent feel? ....

THINK

What options could they try?

Noni could ....

OR she could ....

Wendy could ....

OR she could ....

Brent could ....

OR he could ....

DO

Discuss the consequences of these options.

Choose the option your group thinks is best
If you don't agree, find a compromise; one you will all agree to try.

....

Is this Cool and Friendly? ....

How would they actually DO it?

How would their voices sound?

....

How would their faces look?

....

Where would they stand?

....

Be ready to role-play your chosen DO with your group.

Mastercopy 4: DO Poster

Lesson 17: What friends DO

Outcomes

Students learn to:
> identify skills needed to make and keep friends
> identify 'good bits' about friends
> use STOP THINK DO to solve problems with friends

Resources

STOP THINK DO posters
Worksheet 12 (from previous lesson)
Worksheets 13 and 14
Paper, pencils

Step 1

Social circle

a. Students bring their worksheets from the previous lesson to the circle. Each group of three role-plays its chosen option at DO, sending the right signals in terms of facial expressions, distance and voice to solve the problem.

b. Teacher reinforces students' efforts and shapes their behaviour with guiding comments if they are not quite conveying the right message. Invite students to comment on the role-plays as film directors, offering ideas on voice, face and body cues. While they are role-playing, children may change their minds about their choice of DO or how they DO it because of feedback they receive. This is why practising in groups is so useful!

c. Emphasise that, as with any skill (football, chess, cooking), we can't always get it right the first time we try social skills. We need to get our body into shape and this means practice. And practising our skills in lessons helps us get it right in real life!

d. Fine-tuning our bodies like this so we get it right is just what we need to make and keep friends. Discuss how important friends are throughout our lives. In this lesson we will learn more about what to DO to make and keep friends, and how to DO it!

Step 2

Discussion: Rules for making and keeping friends

a. Remember how we got to know each other better in our early lessons? Ask students to recall rules for meeting and getting to know people since these are the same rules for making friends initially. For example

- Say 'Hello' nicely
- Get eye contact

- Ask questions about the other person to show we are interested
- Listen to their answers, pay attention
- Find things we like that are similar
- Be positive.

b. What extra skills do we need to keep friends once we have made them? Students brainstorm 'What is a friend?' with the group. On the board, draw up a list of things friends DO for and with each other, and what friends DON'T do to each other, for example
- Spend time with them
- Listen to their point of view even if you don't agree
- Accept them even if they make mistakes
- Say and do friendly things for them
- Don't push them around
- Try and help them if they have a problem
- Share and cooperate with them
- Bargain and compromise with them so you both win
- Behave in a Cool and Friendly way with them
- Stand up for yourself but consider their feelings too.

Step 3

Exercise: Handling rejection from a friend

a. Discuss with students how they feel when their friends DON'T do friendly things to or for them? How do they handle rejection by their friends?
b. Fortunately, when friends have problems with each other, they can follow the STOP THINK DO steps to solve it in Cool and Friendly ways.
c. In pairs, students complete Worksheet 13, following the steps on the traffic light posters.

Step 4

Extension activity: Friendliness feedback

In small groups, students get feedback from other students about how good a friend they are, about their 'friendliness'. Students then complete Worksheet 14. This sheet may be re-scored in the future to show students how they are progressing towards friendliness goals.

Worksheet 13: Handling rejection from a friend

STOP

The problem
Your friend ignores you and plays with someone else. You don't know why.

The feelings

You felt ....

Your friend seemed to feel ....

THINK

What could you try?

1. ....

Is this Cool, Weak or Aggro? ....

2. ....

Is this Cool, Weak or Aggro? ....

DO

What might happen if you try these options?

1. ....

2. ....

What would you choose to do?

....

Is it Cool and Friendly? ....

How would you actually DO it?

How would your face look? Sketch it.

....

How would your voice sound?

....

Where would you stand?

....

Don't forget to use STOP THINK DO next time with your friend.

Worksheet 14: Friendliness feedback

Rate your 'friendliness' with the help of opinions from other students.

Friendly things I did or said in the past week

1. ....

2. ....

3. ....

Give myself +1 point for each example.　　　　　　　Total = +　　points

Unfriendly things I said or did in the past week

1. ....

2. ....

3. ....

Give myself −1 point for each example.　　　　　　　Total = −　　points

Friendly things that were said or done to me last week

1. ....

2. ....

3. ....

Give myself +1 point for each example.　　　　　　　Total = +　　points

Unfriendly things that were said or done to me last week

1. ....

2. ....

3. ....

Give myself −1 point for each example.　　　　　　　Total = −　　points

My final friendliness score for this week is ....**points.**

Unit 7: Dealing with unfriendly behaviour

Aims

- To recognise negative pressure, teasing, put downs and physical bullying from others
- To develop emotional control, cognitive and behavioural skills to deal with negative behaviour and pressure from others
- To identify support systems around children when they feel unable to handle negative pressure alone.

Lesson 18: Saying 'No'

Outcomes
Students learn to:
  practise saying 'no' to negative pressure using face, voice and distance cues
  recognise put downs and teasing

Resources
Worksheet 11 (from Lesson 14)
Large sheet of paper or display board
STOP and THINK Friendship video (optional)

Step 1

Social circle

a. Ask students to brainstorm examples of times when they have said 'no' to friends if they don't agree with their actions, comments or requests. Their friends may have been unfair or unreasonable, even if they are friends.
b. As a group, discuss the rules for saying 'No' the Cool way
   - Get eye contact with the person
   - Use a serious face and voice, as if you mean it
   - You don't have to give reasons, but you can
   - You can offer an alternative suggestion, *'Let's do this instead'*
   - If they keep pressuring you or threaten you, say 'No' again and walk away. They are certainly not behaving in a Friendly way
   - If they follow you and keep pressuring you, tell an adult.
c. In small groups, students review their responses on Worksheet 11 involving a very tricky dilemma. They discuss and role-play the Cool way to say 'No' to Ben, using their voice, facial expressions and body position to send the right signals to Ben. Other examples may be selected from the list of social conflicts to discuss, and role-play with fine-tuned bodies.

Step 2

Discussion: Teasing

Ask students to brainstorm examples of put downs and teasing. Suggest that people who put down and tease
  - Hurt someone's feelings
  - Have power over someone
  - Keep it secret to avoid trouble

- Do it repeatedly to wear the person down
- Create a victim.

Alternative resource: *Friendship* video: Teasing

a. Replay Scene 14, p. 57, showing examples of teasing and put downs. Alternatively, students may use the script to role-play the incident themselves.

b. What words describe what is happening to Noni? What are put downs and teasing? Brainstorm ideas. People who put down and tease

- Hurt someone's feelings
- Have power over someone
- Keep it secret to avoid trouble
- Do it repeatedly to wear the person down
- Create a victim.

Step 3

Activity: Group anti-teasing tricks

Introduce the idea that there are Cool techniques to handle teasing. On the board or on paper to retain, draw up three columns as shown below.

STOP	THINK	DO
The problem	What could you try?	**Anti-teasing tricks that work!**
The feelings	What might happen then?	

a. Point to the STOP column. Students give examples of teasing they have experienced or witnessed without mentioning names to blame anyone. Write examples under 'The problem'.

b. Taking one example of teasing at a time, ask students how they would feel if they were teased like that. Record answers under 'The feelings'. It is useful for children to hear that not everyone feels the same about teasing.

c. Point to the THINK column. Students think what they could do if they were teased like that. Record options and discuss possible consequences.

d. In the DO column, children volunteer ideas that have worked for them. Leave list displayed and provide opportunities to add more anti-teasing tricks to it before next lesson.

Teacher note: *The STOP THINK DO process outlined 'de-emotionalises' issues like teasing and reframes them as problem-solving exercises for students. It may be applied to many problems affecting the group, for instance, distracting behaviour.*

Lesson 19: Teasing and bullying

> **Outcomes**
> Students learn to:
> recognise teasing and bullying
> use STOP THINK DO for handling it
> identify people who can assist them
>
> **Resources**
> Anti-teasing tricks (from previous lesson)
> *STOP and THINK Friendship* workbook (optional)

Step 1

Social circle

a. Review the STOP THINK DO list of teasing problems, feelings, options and cool tricks that work. Discuss new anti-teasing tricks added since last lesson. More suggestions are located on p. 36 of the video workbook.

b. Suggest students try tricks from the anti-teasing list when they are teased until they find some that work for them. Discuss possible reminders they can use to try anti-teasing tricks such as wearing or carrying something special.

c. Students plan how to make their anti-teasing tricks into a booklet for distribution to other classes and use by peer mediators as a reference when they are assisting children to deal with teasing in the yard.

d. In summary, Cool ways to cope with teasing generally involve
   - Staying calm, thinking of something nice, counting to 10, singing in your head
   - Ignoring it, walking away, showing it doesn't affect you
   - Doing something the teaser doesn't expect, like laugh, make a joke like Bonez, agree with them or say, 'Pardon, I didn't hear you'.

Step 2

Activity: Popular put downs

a. Discuss how put-downs don't just occur between children. Adults and children also give each other put-downs and criticisms, often without thinking about each other's feelings or the consequences.

b. Students brainstorm examples of popular put-down statements adults make to children. For example
   - You're useless
   - I can't trust you

- Why don't you grow up?
- No wonder no one likes you
- I'd expect that from you
- Why do you bother coming to school?
- Are you deaf?
- Haven't you got a brain?

c. Students brainstorm put downs from children to adults. For example
- You're always picking on me
- It's your fault
- You're always too busy
- I thought you were paid to teach us
- You never listen to me
- Get real
- You just don't understand
- You don't care anyway.

d. Discuss and role-play Cool ways for students to handle put downs from adults
- Stay calm
- Stand straight, get eye contact
- Ignore the put down words, count to 10 or breathe deeply
- If the criticism is justified, apologise and suggest ways to improve
- If it is not justified, firmly but politely explain your position.

Step 3

Discussion: You are not alone

a. As a group, discuss options students have if their anti-teasing tricks don't work in a situation and they become very upset, or if someone is really physically bullying and frightening them. This might occur anywhere. Discuss examples of bullying that students have experienced or witnessed at school, home, sport, in the street, or in the news. Discuss also the consequences that are applied to bullies in our society.

b. Students need to be reassured that they are not expected to handle severe problems alone. Like everyone, they may need assistance at times. Identify 'safe places' and 'safe people' around the school and neighbourhood for students to go to if necessary. Particularly, outline the process children follow in your school to get help.

Lesson 20: We can STOP THINK DO! Yahoo!

Outcomes

Students learn to:
- use co-operative skills to organise a class party
- set tasks and follow through with plans
- review their progress
- celebrate!

Resources

Worksheet 1 (second review)
Pencils, Textas
Co-operation *Rules*! poster (optional, from Lesson 15)
Worksheet 15
Parent Information 3
STOP and THINK Friendship video (optional); p.38 of workbook (optional)

Step 1

Social circle

a. We have all learned so much about social skills since we began the STOP THINK DO lessons. What have we learned? Review skills for STOP (using eyes and ears to work out feelings and problems), THINK (using brains to solve problems) and DO (fine-tuning bodies to send the right signals).

b. What have we learned about each other? Remind students of the 'good bits' that have been identified by teacher and classmates. We learned that we can work very well together as a group using STOP THINK DO.

Step 2

Exercise: Have I improved?

Students refer to Worksheet 1 for a review of their progress towards achieving the goals set in Lesson 4. They record positive comments that have been made about them by others, and their opinions. They may set further goals to achieve.

Step 3

Activity: Graduation certificate

Students design their own graduation certificates with computer or pencils, to be formally presented at the party. Alternatively, certificates from p. 38 of the video workbook may be coloured by students.

Additional resource: *Friendship* video: Party time!

Show the party, Scene 17, p. 58. Yes, even Bonez makes mistakes and forgets to use STOP THINK DO sometimes! The students will also make mistakes and go back to their old habits sometimes. But if they use reminders and keep cool, they will get it right more often. They will get on better with others and feel better about themselves. STOP THINK DO is a good habit they can use all of their life! And, now that they have graduated, they could take over Bonez's job in the Friendship Neighbourhood!

Step 4

Activity: Planning our party!

a. Now it is time to plan our party! Remember our Co-operation *Rules!* poster, using Cool and Friendly ways to work in groups? We will need to use these skills to work together and plan our party. If poster is not available, remind students of the rules for co-operation, that is, Cool + Friendly behaviour.

b. First we identify the tasks that will need to be done for the party to be a success. Teacher offers suggestions as students brainstorm ideas, such as

- What is the date of the party?
- Where will we have it?
- Who will we invite?
- Will our parents come to the party?
- Who will design the invitations?
- What will we eat?
- What music will we have?
- What decorations shall we have?
- Who will take the photos?
- Who will clean up?

c. Hand out Worksheet 15. Divide the class into groups of four. Assign a different task to each group. Discuss a timeline and a review date to keep them on track. Each group completes the worksheet to clarify their task.

d. The school principal may be invited to the party to officially hand out certificates to students. The successful completion of the program and the final celebration may be reported in the school newsletter and local paper.

Teacher note: *The model of a cooperative group plan on Worksheet 15 may be used in many situations where the class needs to work together on a group task, including a cooperative learning task.*

Parent information

Distribute Parent Information 3 for students to take home to their parents with a note about the party, along with their Social Skills folders for parental feedback.

Worksheet 17: Planning our party!

Use STOP THINK DO to help you work in your small group on the big task of planning our class graduation party.

STOP — **What is the task your small group has in planning our class party?**

....

How do you feel about this task?

....

THINK — **What things does your group have to do to complete their task? Who will do them?**

1. ....
....

2. ....
....

3. ....
....

4. ....
....

DO — **Do these things until your group's task is completed by the set date, which is**

....

Then we can all enjoy the party!

Parent Information 3: What your child is learning

In STOP THINK DO social skills lessons, the children are currently learning

- To choose to behave in ways that have the best consequences
- To practise behavioural skills that send the right signals to others
- To remember the green traffic light as a cue to DO these skills
- To make and keep friends
- To handle negative pressure, put downs, teasing and bullying
- To identify support systems around them if they need help
- To cooperate as a class on projects, like planning a graduation party.

What can you do to help your child learn these valuable skills?

- When children are learning new skills, it is very helpful for their parents to talk with them about what they are learning
- Parents can also look for and praise any positive changes in their child's behaviour and attitudes
- You may check your child's Social Skills folder and discuss the exercises with your child. This folder needs to be returned to school for review purposes.

Since the formal social skills lessons are now finished, your child has graduated from the program and will participate in a class party on

....

We are asking for your help to make the party a success by providing

....

....

Appendix

Appendix

CONTENTS OF APPENDIX

- Teacher training exercise: Bad habits — 200
- Teacher training exercise: Stop, look and listen instead — 201
- Teacher training exercise: Manage the behaviour — 202
- STOP THINK DO peer mediation checklist — 204
- Parents' introduction to STOP THINK DO — 206
- Social problems for discussion and role-play — 207
- Teacher assessment of social skills: PRE form — 208
- Student assessment of social skills: PRE form — 209
- Teacher assessment of social skills: POST form — 210
- Student assessment of social skills: POST form — 211
- STOP THINK DO resources — 213
- References — 215

Teacher training exercise: Bad habits

Consider these scenarios where adults don't STOP first when managing children, but act impulsively and emotionally.

1. *Nine-year-old Johnny is a likeable boy although young for his age in terms of taking responsibility. He is disorganised and relies on others to help him.*

Teacher (friendly tone)	'Please put your homework on the table for marking.'
Johnny (hesitantly)	'Oh, I left my book at home.'
Teacher (frustrated tone)	'Sure, you seem to be forgetting *everything* lately, Johnny.'
Johnny (upset)	'It's not my fault. Mum forgot to put my book in my bag.'

What did this teacher assume about Johnny? ....

How did she feel? ....

How did she express her feelings? ....

How did the child respond then? ....

Notes: Johnny is a dependent personality who relies on others rather than taking responsibility himself. Did this teacher inadvertently reinforce his dependency and immaturity by her rather sarcastic tone, which prompted him to defend himself in his usual dependent way, namely, by blaming someone else?

2. *Fourteen-year-old Maria runs excitedly into the kitchen, where her parents are chatting.*

Maria (cheerfully)	'Can I have $5 advance on my allowance for the disco?'
Father (accusingly)	'What do you do with your money? I bet you waste it on drugs like your useless friends.'
Maria (defiantly)	'How dare you say that about my friends! Anyway, you're the meanest parents in the world.'
Father (angrily)	'Don't you speak to us like that. That's typical of you teenagers these days. You won't get any money from us!'
Maria (stubbornly)	'Well, I'll just have to get it another way.'
	She storms out and later takes $5 from mother's purse and lies to go to the disco.

What did the father assume? ....

How did he feel? ....

How did he express his feelings? ....

How did the child respond? ....

Notes: Maria is a power personality who needs to have control in her life. Did her father actually initiate a power struggle and revenge cycle in the family by reacting emotionally and abusively to her, which prompted her to fight back to get her own needs met?

Teacher training exercise: Stop, look and listen instead

Consider an alternative approach to the problems in the previous exercise.

1. Johnny's teacher stops, looks and listens in the beginning of the interaction about his maths homework in order to clarify the facts of the situation, without guessing or making assumptions.

What would she have actually seen and heard happen regarding the maths book?

....

....

Of course, she still may have felt frustrated.
But, how could she have expressed her feelings and concerns appropriately, rather than putting Johnny down?

'I feel ………………….. because ……………………………………………….'

Notes: Would this approach be less likely to trigger defensive and dependent reactions in Johnny, and more likely to open the door for teacher and Johnny to work out ways to help him remember his homework?

2. Maria's father stops, looks and listens in the beginning of this interaction with his daughter in order to get the facts clear, without guessing or assuming.

What would he have actually seen and heard happen regarding the money?

....

....

He may still have felt worried or concerned.
But how could he have expressed his feelings and concerns appropriately without attacking everything important to his daughter?

'I feel ………………….. because ……………………………………………….'

Notes: Would this approach be less likely to trigger a power struggle with Maria, and more likely to open the door for father and Maria to work out issues like her budget?

Teacher training exercise: Manage the behaviour

Consider this typical classroom problem

Joseph is a very loud, active boy in your class. While you are explaining a new concept to another child, you hear him tapping his ruler on the table and singing behind you, evoking quite a reaction from his classmates, especially Chloe, whom he annoys.

How would you feel? ……………………………………………………………………

What would you impulsively do? ……………………………………………………………

Could your reaction actually reinforce Joseph's misbehaviour, for instance, by giving him attention?

Now, solve this problem using STOP THINK DO.

STOP
Use your eyes and ears to find out what actually happened in the beginning

……………………………………………………………………………………………………

Express your feelings as the teacher appropriately in an I- message

'I feel …………………… because ………………………..…………………………….'

THINK
What options could you try to solve this problem?

1. ……………………………………………………………………………………………

2. ……………………………………………………………………………………………

3. ……………………………………………………………………………………………

What are the likely consequences of these options?

1. ……………………………………………………………………………………………

2. ……………………………………………………………………………………………

3. ……………………………………………………………………………………………

DO
Choose the option with the most acceptable consequences

....

BUT could this option also have the consequence of emphasising Joseph's 'bad bits'?

Notes: Another option might be *group* problem solving to avoid singling out Joseph. In such a scenario the class brainstorms options for solving the less personalised problem of 'What can we do when people distract us in our class?'. The group then chooses an option to try and puts it into action with a review time set to make adjustments if necessary and avoid failure.

STOP THINK DO PEER MEDIATION CHECKLIST

Step 1   Peer mediators outline the ground rules for the mediation to all parties.

Step 2   **STOP**   *What is the problem?*

Record how Party 1 sees the problem.

....

....

Step 3   Ask Party 2 to repeat what they heard Party 1 say.

Step 4   Record how Party 2 sees the problem.

....

....

Step 5   Ask Party 1 to repeat what they heard Party 2 say.

Step 6   **THINK** *What are some suggestions from both parties to solve this problem and the likely consequences for each suggestion?*

Suggested options	Likely consequences
1.	
2.	

3.	
4.	

Discuss each option and the possible consequences for both parties.

Step 7 **DO** *Which option do you both agree would be the best to try?*

Record the chosen option.

....

....

Step 8 Both parties sign the agreement to put the plan into action.
Set a review time if both parties agree.
At ....

....
Party 1 Signature   Party 2 Signature

Parents' introduction to STOP THINK DO

Date

Dear parents

We are about to run a social skills training program called STOP THINK DO at school.

The aim of the program is to develop a more positive classroom and schoolyard environment for all students. Children also learn better when they are getting on well with other students and their teachers.

The program teaches children to
- Listen to and talk with others
- Understand other people's feelings
- Express their own feelings appropriately
- STOP and THINK before they act, and thus
- Make good decisions and choices
- Make and keep friends
- Stand up for themselves positively
- Cope with teasing and negative pressure
- Work in groups and help each other
- Feel better about themselves, their class and their school

Parents are an important part of this program. They can help their children learn and practise these skills by looking for positive changes in their children's attitude or behaviour, and praising them for it.

During the program, the students will bring home current information about what they are learning and also their Social Skills folders to show parents. Please look at this information with your child and talk to them about it.

If you wish to discuss the program further with the teacher, please make an appointment. Information about STOP THINK DO may also be obtained on the website *www.stopthinkdo.com*.

....
Teacher   Principal

Social problems for discussion and role-play

Teachers may select stories from this list to present to students for discussion and role-play in social skills lessons and for spontaneous practice and review at other times. Teachers may enlarge on the characters and themes themselves, or encourage students to do so by brainstorming ideas to fill out the story, and/or writing a story script including dialogue for the characters.

- Another student keeps laughing at you and annoying you in class, even though you are trying to get on with your work.
- You have a friend over who trashes your room and refuses to help you clean it up.
- Your sister wants to watch a cartoon and you want to play video games on the TV.
- Your mother won't let you play on the computer until you feed your pets.
- Your teacher said you can't sit next to your best friend because you talk too much. But you really have been trying to work well lately.
- A classmate mentioned her birthday party to you but forgot to give you an invitation.
- You have a new skateboard and your friend keeps asking to borrow it. You know she is rough with things.
- Your best friend is playing with a group and ignores you when you ask if you can join them.
- You have just watched a scary movie and you have to go bed alone. Your sister laughs at you.
- Your teacher hands back your English test. Your mark is very low. The student next to you has received the top mark.
- You are helping your dad set the table. You smash one of the family's best dinner plates.
- You have finally finished your homework and done it well. Your little brother spills orange juice all over it.
- You are walking around the house complaining that there is nothing to do. Your neighbour suggests that you smash bottles in the shed.
- You are looking everywhere for your pet dog which is lost. Your sister helps you look for it and she finds it.
- You lied to your father about going to the pop concert, and he found out the truth.
- You borrow your brother's favourite T-shirt to wear at the weekend and you get a hole in it.
- The friends that you hang around with at school don't want you in their group any more and you don't know why.
- Your sister has her CD player very loud while you are trying to do your homework in the next room.
- Your mother has grounded you because you got in trouble at school but you really want to go to the football.
- You have been good friends with Paul for a long time but now other friends are teasing you about Paul being your boyfriend.
- You really don't like smoking cigarettes because they are dangerous to your health, but your friends say you're weak for not smoking.

Teacher assessment of social skills: PRE form

Name _____ Date _____

School _____ Class _____

Code: 1 = Never; 2 = Rarely; 3 = Sometimes; 4 = Usually; 5 = Always.

Please circle the appropriate number. Is the student

1. **Accepted or liked by their peers?**

    1   2   3   4   5

2. **Attention seeking/demanding?**

    1   2   3   4   5

3. **Verbally aggressive?**

    1   2   3   4   5

4. **Physically aggressive?**

    1   2   3   4   5

5. **Outgoing and confident?**

    1   2   3   4   5

6. **Able to appropriately assert themselves when teased?**

    1   2   3   4   5

7. **Having difficulty making friends?**

    1   2   3   4   5

8. **Having difficulty keeping friends?**

    1   2   3   4   5

9. **Impulsive?**

    1   2   3   4   5

Student assessment of social skills: PRE form

Name _____ Date _____

School _____ Class _____

Please circle the answer that is true for you

1. **How much are you liked by other children?**

    Not at all   A little bit   Quite a lot   Heaps

2. **Do you fight with other children?**

    Not at all   A little bit   Quite a lot   Heaps

3. **Are you shy with other children?**

    Not at all   A little bit   Quite a lot   Heaps

4. **Does teasing upset you?**

    Not at all   A little bit   Quite a lot   Heaps

5. **Is it hard for you to make friends?**

    Not at all   A little bit   Quite a lot   Heaps

6. **Is it hard for you to keep your friends?**

    Not at all   A little bit   Quite a lot   Heaps

7. **Do you get on with your teacher?**

    Not at all   A little bit   Quite a lot   Heaps

Teacher assessment of social skills: POST form

Name _____ Date _____

School _____ Class _____

Code: 1 = Never; 2 = Rarely; 3 = Sometimes; 4 = Usually; 5 = Always.

Please circle the appropriate number. Is the student

1. **Accepted or liked by their peers?**

    1   2   3   4   5

2. **Attention seeking/demanding?**

    1   2   3   4   5

3. **Verbally aggressive?**

    1   2   3   4   5

4. **Physically aggressive?**

    1   2   3   4   5

5. **Outgoing and confident?**

    1   2   3   4   5

6. **Able to appropriately assert themselves when teased?**

    1   2   3   4   5

7. **Having difficulty making friends?**

    1   2   3   4   5

8. **Having difficulty keeping friends?**

    1   2   3   4   5

9. **Impulsive?**

    1   2   3   4   5

Student assessment of social skills: POST form

Name _____ Date _____

School _____ Class _____

Please circle the answer that is true for you

1. **How much are you liked by other children?**

    Not at all   A little bit   Quite a lot   Heaps

2. **Do you fight with other children?**

    Not at all   A little bit   Quite a lot   Heaps

3. **Are you shy with other children?**

    Not at all   A little bit   Quite a lot   Heaps

4. **Does teasing upset you?**

    Not at all   A little bit   Quite a lot   Heaps

5. **Is it hard for you to make friends?**

    Not at all   A little bit   Quite a lot   Heaps

6. **Is it hard for you to keep your friends?**

    Not at all   A little bit   Quite a lot   Heaps

7. **Do you get on with your teacher?**

    Not at all   A little bit   Quite a lot   Heaps

STOP THINK DO RESOURCES

Other STOP THINK DO resources

Petersen, L. & Adderley, A. (2002). *STOP THINK DO Social Skills Training: Early years of schooling, ages 4–8.* Australian Council for Educational Research, Victoria.

Petersen, L. (2002). *STOP THINK DO Posters.* Australian Council for Educational Research, Victoria.

Petersen, L. (2002). *STOP and THINK Parenting*, 2nd edition, Australian Council for Educational Research, Victoria.

Petersen, L. & LeMessurier, M. (2000). *STOP and THINK Friendship* video package. Foundation Studios, Adelaide, South Australia.

Petersen, L. (1995). *STOP and THINK Learning: A teacher's guide for motivating children to learn including those with special needs.* Australian Council for Educational Research, Victoria.

STOP THINK DO web site: *www.stopthinkdo.com*

Earlier publications no longer in print

Adderley, A., Petersen, L. & Gannoni, A. F. (1997). *Social Skills Training: First 3 years of schooling.* Australian Council for Educational Research, Victoria.

Petersen, L. & Gannoni, A. F. (1992). *Teachers' Manual for Training Social Skills while Managing Student Behaviour.* Australian Council for Educational Research, Victoria.

Petersen, L. & Gannoni, A. F. (1991). *Manual for Social Skills Training in Young People with Parent and Teacher Programs.* Australian Council for Educational Research, Victoria.

REFERENCES

Andary, L. (1990). An evaluation of the Adelaide Children's Hospital's cognitive-behavioural social skills program. Unpublished Master of Psychology thesis, Flinders University of South Australia.

Asher, S. R. & Rose, A. J. (1997). In Salovey, P. & Sluyter, D. J. (eds) *Emotional development and emotional intelligence: Educational implications,* 196–230. Basic Books Inc., New York.

Bagwell, C. L., Newcomb, A. F. & Bukowski, W. M. (1998). Preadolescent friendship and peer rejection as predictors of adult adjustment. *Child Development*, Vol. 69(1), 140–53.

Barrett, P., Turner, C., Rombouts, S. & Duffy, A. (2000). Reciprocal skills training in the treatment of externalising behaviour disorders in childhood: A preliminary investigation. *Behaviour Change,* Vol. 17, No. 4, 221–34.

Beck, J. & Horne, D. (1992). A whole school implementation of the Stop, Think Do! social skills training program at Minerva Special School. In Willis, B. & Izard, J. F. (eds) *Student Behaviour Problems: Directions, Perspectives and Expectations*. Australian Council for Educational Research, Victoria.

Bierman, K. L. & Greenberg, M. T. (1996). In Ray DeV. Peters, R. DeV. & McMahon, R.J. (eds) *Preventing childhood disorders, substance abuse, and delinquency,* 65–89. Sage Publications, Inc., CA, USA.

Bierman, K. L. (1996). In Ferris, C. F. & Grisso, T. (eds) *Understanding aggressive behaviour in children,* 256–64. New York Academy of Sciences, New York.

Bulkeley, R. & Cramer, D. (1994). Social skills training with young adolescents: Group and individual approaches in a school setting. *Journal of Adolescence*, Vol. 17, 521–31.

Bullock, J. R. (1992). Children without friends: Who are they and how can teachers help? *Childhood Education*, Vol. 69(2), 92–6.

Cocco, K. M. (1995). Social cognitive factors related to adjustment in school age children. *Dissertation Abstracts International: Section B: The Sciences and Engineering*, Vol. 56(3-B), 1717.

Coie, J. D. & Koeppl, G. K. (1990). Adapting intervention to the problems of aggressive and disruptive rejected children. In Asher, S. R. & Coie, J. D. (eds), *Peer rejection in childhood,* 309–37, Cambridge University Press, Cambridge, UK.

Coie, J. D., Terry, R., Lenox, K. & Lochman, J. (1995). Childhood peer rejection and aggression as predictors of stable patterns of adolescent disorder. *Development and Pychopathology,* Vol. 7, 697–713.

Corrie, L. & Leitao, N. (1999). The development of wellbeing: Young children's knowledge of their support networks and social competence. *Australian Journal of Early Childhood,* Sept, Vol. 24(3), 25.

Cousins L. S. & Weiss, G. (1993). Parent training and social skills training for children with attention-deficit hyperactivity disorder: How can they be combined for greater effectiveness? *Canadian Journal of Psychiatry,* Aug, Vol. 38, 449–57.

Day, P., Murphy, A. & Cooke, J. (1999). Traffic light lessons: problem solving skills with adolescents. *Community Practitioner,* Oct, Vol. 72, No. 10, 322–4.

Eisenberg, N., Guthrie, I. K., Fabes, R. A., Reiser, M. & Murphy, B.C. (1997). The relations of regulation and emotionality to resiliency and competent social functioning in elementary school children. *Child Development,* Vol. 68, 295–311.

Elias, M. & Weissberg, R. (1990). School-based social competence promotion as a primary prevention strategy: A tale of two projects. *Prevention in Human Services,* Vol. 7(1), 177–85.

Farmer-Dougan, V., Viechtbauer, W, & French, T. (1999). Peer-prompted social skills: The role of teacher consultation in student success. *Educational Psychology*, Jun, Vol. 19(2), 207–19.

Frey, K. S., Hirschstein, M. K., & Guzzo, B. A. (2000). Second step: Preventing aggression by promoting social competence. *Journal of Emotional and Behavioral Disorders*, Vol. 8(2), 102–12.

Frankel, F., Myatt, R., Cantwell, D. P. & Feinberg, D. T. (1997). Parent-assisted transfer of children's social skills training: Effects on children with and without attention-deficit hyperactivity disorder. *Journal of American Academy of Child and Adolescent Psychiatry,* Aug, Vol. 36(8), 1056–64.

Gibbs, J. C., Granville, B., Barriga, A. Q. & Liau, A. K. (1996). Developing the helping skills and prosocial motivation of aggressive adolescents in peer group programs. *Aggression & Violent Behaviour,* Fall, Vol. 1(3), 283–305.

Goleman, D. (1997). *Emotional Intelligence: Why it can matter more than IQ*. Bantam Books New York.

Gumpel, T. P. & Frank, R. (1999). An expansion of the peer-tutoring paradigm: Cross-age peer tutoring of social skills among socially rejected boys. *Journal of Applied Behavior Analysis*, Vol. 32, 115–18.

Harbeitner, M. H. (1997). The effects of social skills and peer/parent facilitation generalization training on the impulsive, aggressive, and noncompliant behaviour of peer-rejected students diagnosed with attention deficit disorder. *Dissertation Abstracts International Section A: Humanities & Social Sciences,* May, Vol. 57(11-A), 4647.

Hymel, S., Rubin, K. H., Rowden, L. & LeMare, L. (1990). Children's peer relationships: Longitudinal prediction of internalising and externalising problems from middle to late childhood. *Child Development*, Vol. 61, 2004–21.

Howes, C. (2000). Social-emotional classroom climate in child care, child-teacher relationships and children's second grade peer relations. *Social Development*, Vol. 9(2), 191–204.

Jones, R. N., Sheridan, S. M. & Binns, W. R. (1993). Schoolwide social skills training: Providing preventive services to students at-risk. *School Psychology Quarterly*, Spring, Vol. 8(1), 57–80.

Kazdin, A. E., Siegal, T. C. & Bass, D. (1992). Cognitive problem-solving skills training and parent management training in the treatment of antisocial behaviour in children. *Journal of Consulting and Clinical Psychology*, Vol. 60, 733–47.

Kim, H. (1996). The effects of combined self-management strategies on the generalization of social behaviour changes in children with social skills deficits. *Dissertation Abstracts International Section A: Humanities & Social Sciences,* Vol. 56(8-A), 3079.

Kohler, F. W. & Strain, P. S. (1999). Maximising peer-mediated resources in integrated preschool classrooms. *Topics in Early Childhood Special Education,* Summer, Vol. 19(2), 92.

Ladd, G. W. (1990). Having friends, keeping friends, making friends, and being liked by peers in the classroom: Predictors of children's early school adjustment. *Child Development*, Vol. 61, 1081–100.

Ladd, G. W. (1999). Peer relationships and social competence during early and middle childhood. *Annual Review of Psychology*, Vol. 1, 333.

Ladd, G. W., Kochenderfer, B. J. & Coleman, C. C. (1996). Friendship quality as a predictor of young children's early school adjustment. *Child Development*, Vol. 67(3), 1103–18.

La Greca, A. M. (1993). Social skills training with children: Where do we go from here? *Journal of Clinical Child Psychology*, Vol. 22(1), 288–98.

Lawhorn, T. (1997). Encouraging friendships among children. *Childhood Education*, Vol. 73(4), 228–33.

Lease, A. M. (1995). Cognitive and motivational influences on children's social competence and social adjustment. *Dissertation Abstracts International: Section B: The Sciences & Engineering,* Sep, Vol. 56(3-B), 1703.

Lowenthal, B. (1996). Teaching social skills to preschoolers with special needs. *Childhood Education*, Spring, Vol. 72(3), 137(4).

Lowry-Webster, H. M., Barrett, P. & Dadds, M. R. (2001). A universal prevention trial of anxiety and depressive symptomatology in childhood: Preliminary data from an Australian study. *Behaviour Change,* Vol. 18(1), 36–50.

Matthys, W., Cuperus, J. M & van Engeland, H. (1999). Deficient social problem-solving in boys with ODD/CD, with ADHD, and with both disorders. *Journal of American Academy of Child and Adolescent Psychiatry,* March, Vol. 38(3), 311–21.

Newcomb, A. F. & Bagwell, C. L. (1998). The developmental significance of children's friendship relations. In Bukowski, W. A., Newcomb, A. F. & Hartup, W. W. (eds), *The company they keep: Friendship in childhood and adolescence*. Cambridge University Press, New York.

Nimmo, J. (1993). Social competence: A pilot study of a cognitive-behavioural social skills program with comparisons of outcomes for in-class and withdrawal groups. Unpublished Master of Education thesis, Queensland University.

Ogilvy, C. M. (1994). Social skills training with children and adolescents: A review of the evidence on effectiveness. *Educational Psychology*, Vol. 14(1) 73–83.

Parkhurst, J. T. & Asher, S. R. (1985). Goals and concerns: Implications for the study of children's social competence. In Lahey, B. B. & Kazdin, A. E. (eds), *Advances in Clinical Child Psychology,* Vol. 8, Plenum Press, New York.

Pepler, D. J., King, G., Graig, W., Byrd, B. & Bream, L. (1995). The development and evaluation of a multisystem social skills training program for aggressive children. *Child and Youth Care Forum*, Oct, Vol. 24(5), 297–313.

Pfiffner, L. J. & McBurnett, K. (1997). Social skills training with parent generalization: Treatment effects for children with attention deficit disorder. *Journal of Consulting and Clinical Psychology,* Vol. 65(5), 749–57.

Pianta, R. C. (1997). Adult-child relationship processes and early schooling. *Early Education and Development*, Vol. 8, 11–26.

Puskar, K. R., Lamb, J. & Tusaie-Mumford, K. (1997). Teaching kids to cope: A preventive mental health nursing strategy for adolescents. *Journal of Child and Adolescent Psychiatric Nursing,* July–Sept, Vol. 10(3), 18–30.

Simpson, R. L. & Smith Myles, B. (1998). Aggression among children and youth who have Asperger's Syndrome: A different population requiring different strategies. *Preventing School Failure,* Summer, Vol. 42(4), 149–56.

Spence, S. H. & Donovan, C. (1998). *Cognitive-behaviour therapy for children and families,* 217–45. Cambridge University Press, New York.

Strayhorn, J. M., Strain, P. S. & Walker, H. M. (1993). The case for interaction skills training in the context of tutoring as a preventive mental health intervention in schools. *Behavioral Disorders*, Vol. 19(1), 11–26.

Tankersley, M., Kamps, D., Mancina, C. & Weidinger, D. (1996). Social interventions for head start children with behavioral risks: Implementation and outcomes. *Journal of Emotional and Behavioral Disorders*, Vol. 4(3), 171–81.

Thompson, K. L., Bundy, K. A. & Wolfe, W. R. (1996). Social skills training for young adolescents: Cognitive and performance components. *Adolescence,* Fall, Vol. 31(123), 505(17).

Vitaro, F. & Tremblay, R. E. (1994). Impact of a prevention program on aggressive children's friendships and social adjustment. *Journal of Abnormal Child Psychology*, Vol. 22(4), 457–72.

Wentzel, K. R. & Caldwell, K. (1997). Friendship, peer acceptance, and group membership: Relations to academic achievement in middle school. *Child Development*, Vol. 68(6), 1198–209.

Stop Think Do: Social Skills Training Primary Years of Schooling Ages 4-8

STOP THINK DO is an Australian social skills program for use in schools with children who have emotional–social–behavioural difficulties that affect their ability to make friends. It is also designed as a classroom curriculum for children to prevent such difficulties arising.

Stop Think Do: Social Skills Training Primary Years of Schooling Ages 4-8 engages junior primary students with fun STOP THINK DO games and activities, cute illustrations, and encourages confidence during these formative years.

This revised and extended edition modernises this best-selling program, incorporating current research trends, visual resources, simplified lesson formats and practical suggestions for applying the program in regular classrooms, in small groups, for special needs students, for peer mediators, or as a whole school. Parental involvement is also encouraged.

RRP $89.95
Cat. No. A300HG
ISBN 0-86431-536-8

Stop and Think Parenting

This is the second edition of Lindy Petersen's popular parenting resource. Based on her STOP THINK DO method of teaching social skills to children, Lindy explores the benefits of sharing with your child, the rights and responsibilities of living in a family.

Stop and Think Parenting teaches parents and children to manage situations and avoid knee-jerk reactions when children behave in a way that upsets parents and other children, by thinking about the behaviour and what can be done to change or prevent it.

RRP $19.95
Cat. No. A998BK
ISBN 0-86431-560-0

To purchase these new titles by Lindy Petersen, please contact ACER Press' customer service department;

ACER Press
347 Camberwell Road
(Private Bag 55)
Camberwell VIC 3124

Tel: 03 9835 7447
Fax: 03 9835 7449
e-mail: sales@acer.edu.au

or visit ACER online at;

www.acer.edu.au

'The examples discussed by Lindy were insightful and helpful in understanding the issues facing teachers and their students.'

'Great practical suggestions, many avenues to explore.'

'A most worthwhile day! Great food for thought.'

'Many thanks for a worthwhile and stimulating day.'

'I enjoyed your case study stories.'

STOP THINK DO

A program for motivating children's social and learning skills presented by Lindy Petersen

This session introduces the STOP THINK DO program to support parents and classroom teachers in the development of:
Social skills training for children,
Behaviour guidance strategies, and
Motivating children's learning.

Workshop Outline
Introduction to STOP THINK DO program
Development of the program
The STOP THINK DO process using the traffic light cues
Programs to create good learning environments in classrooms
Application of learning plans for children with special needs
Reflection and further questions

To register for Lindy Petersen's next STOP THINK DO workshop, or to find out more about ACER's professional development program, please contact the Professional Development Unit;

ACER Professional Development Unit
347 Camberwell Road
(Private Bag 55)
Camberwell VIC 3124

Tel: 03 9835 7403
Fax: 03 9835 7457
e-mail: workshops@acer.edu.au

or visit ACER online at;

www.acer.edu.au